THE DIARY OF
MICHAEL WIGGLESWORTH
1653-1657

The Conscience of a Puritan

Edited by
EDMUND S. MORGAN

HARPER TORCHBOOKS   The Academy Library
Harper & Row, Publishers, New York

THE DIARY OF MICHAEL WIGGLESWORTH 1653–1657

THE DIARY OF
MICHAEL WIGGLESWORTH
1653-1657

harper 🔥 torchbooks

*A reference-list of Harper Torchbooks, classified
by subjects, is printed at the end of this volume.*

THE DIARY OF
MICHAEL WIGGLESWORTH
1653-1657

INTRODUCTION

The Author

We have been discovering in recent years that the Puritans were much more human than we had once supposed. They ate and drank and fought and loved and even occasionally laughed a little. Perhaps then they were (like us) hearty, warm-hearted creatures after all. Perhaps. When we begin to think of the Puritans this way, we sooner or later have to reckon with a man like Michael Wigglesworth. The grim pages of his *Day of Doom* have long been familiar to students of American literature. His diary is even more more challenging than his verse to any liberal view of the Puritans. For the man that emerges here calls to mind those stern figures in steeple-crowned hats who represent Puritanism in popular cartoons. So closely does Michael Wigglesworth approximate the unhappy popular conception of our seventeenth-century forbears that he seems more plausible as a satirical reconstruction than he does as a human being. His very name, to anyone not familiar with its illustrious history, must suggest a caricature, and the suggestion is sadly borne out by the diary and supported by all that can be ascertained about him.

His biography, as we know it from other sources than the diary, is appropriate. He was one of the first settlers of New England; he attended Harvard, the Puritan college, and taught there for several years (during which he wrote most of this diary); he became a minister and spent the greater part of his life preaching Puritanism to the people of Malden, Massachusetts. He wrote a poem which his fellow-Puritans bought by the thousands in order to read in vivid figures about the Day of Judgment. In keeping with the crabbed figure of the cartoon, he was a sickly man, always complaining of ill health; throughout a large part of his life he was an invalid. Yet he fathered eight children, outlived two wives, and had married a third when he died in 1705 in his seventy-fourth year.[1]

[1] Further details of Wigglesworth's biography may be found in John W. Dean, *Memoir of the Reverend Michael Wigglesworth* (Albany, 1871) and in Richard Crowder, *No Featherbed to Heaven: A Biography of Michael Wigglesworth, 1631-1705* (East Lansing, Michigan, 1962).

The pattern was not an uncommon one among the first generation of New Englanders: Harvard, the ministry, the ripe and respected old age. Against this familiar backdrop the diary fills in the lines of the caricature with heavy strokes, until the Puritan emerges as his worst enemies would have him, a man with great capacity for survival—but with small reason for wanting to survive. Was the Puritan a killjoy? Wigglesworth thought that all pleasure apart from delight in God's grace was dangerous. His heart was "sunk with sorrow" when he found his students at Harvard indulging in merriment. Thus he wrote on June 25, 1653:

> I set my self again this day to wrestle with the Lord for my self and then for my pupils and the Lord did pretty much inlarge my heart in crying to him. But still I see the Lord shutting out my prayers and refusing to hear for he whom in special I pray'd for, I heard in the forenoon with ill company playing musick, though I had so solemnly warn'd him but yesterday of letting his spirit go after pleasures. (p. 27)

Since the students at Harvard could not fail to display a certain amount of animal spirits, this type of experience continued to sadden the teacher's heart. On one occasion he gave a delinquent student a long lecture on the dangers of pleasure, and yet "that very evening," Wigglesworth confided to the diary, "he was again at play . . . and when he saw me coming he slinked home and left his game whereby I gather that he is more afraid of me a poor sinful worm than of God and I am sorry that so solemn a warning and so efficacious for the present should have lost its power so soon." (p. 27) Wigglesworth had no appreciation for the humor in situations of this kind, and he suffered the most innocuous pranks of his students with a ludicrous air of mourning. When he heard some of his admonitions "with derision reiterated among the scolars," he solemnly sought comfort in his Maker. (p. 39) And when the students displayed a not incomprehensible reluctance to study Hebrew, he saw in their intractability "A spirit of unbridled licentiousness," and exclaimed, "Lord in mercy heal, or I know not what wil become of New England." (p. 67).

If worrying would have saved New England, Wigglesworth would have saved it. One of the most revealing passages in the diary is the one where he records his almost ridiculously painful deliberations about a neighbor's door swinging back and forth in the wind.

> The wise god who knoweth how to tame and take down proud and wanton hearts, suffereth me to be sorely buffeted with the like tempta-

tion as formerly about seeing some dores blow to and fro with the wind in some danger to break, as I think; I cannot tel whether it were my duty to giue them some hint that owe them. When I think 'tis a common thing, and that 'tis impossible but that the owners should haue oft seen them in that case, and heard them blow to and fro, and that it is but a trivial matter, and that I haue given a hint to one that dwels in the hous, and he maketh light of it; and that it would rather be a seeming to check others mindlesness of their own affairs, and lastly that there may be special reasons for it that I know not; why the case seemeth clear that 'tis not my duty. yet I am sorely affraid I should regard iniquity in my heart, and god upon this ecclypseth the sweet beam's of his love, he hideth his face and I am troubled. (p. 71)

Wigglesworth worried not only about his neighbors' doors but also, of course, about their souls. He found his spirit "quite discouraged and soul and body both ready to quail, because of my sorrows for what mine eyes daly behould in others sins and mispense of their precious hours." (p. 29) He resolved "to do more for christ than I haue done by reproveing lightness and mad mirth on Sabbath Evenings and by visitings." (p. 66) He even became so concerned with saving the souls of others that he found it necessary to reprimand himself for having, as he said, "a greater desire of others finding christ than of my own." (p. 64)

In strange company with this solicitude went an unrestrained selfishness, which is revealed in a remarkable series of reflections on marriage. Wigglesworth evidently believed that he was suffering from gonorrhea and accordingly had some doubts about whether or not he should marry. His doubts arose, however, not from any concern for his bride-to-be, but from an apprehension that marriage might impair his own health. The factor which finally determined him to marry was the advice of a physician that marriage might prove beneficial, instead of detrimental. He accordingly resolved "to redeem the spring time for marrying or taking physick or both." (p.85) The sad sequel is that his bride died four years after her marriage, from what cause is unknown.

His crass behavior in this episode never gave Wigglesworth any pangs of conscience, but he was by no means free from a morbid feeling of guilt for other offenses that we should probably consider entirely innocuous. Guilt, in fact, seems to have been a necessary feeling to Wigglesworth. The diary served as a kind of account-book in which he rendered up the assets and liabilities of his soul, with the debit side of the ledger receiving almost all the entries. It was not that he ever behaved in a scandalous fashion outwardly; his outward behavior was doubtless exemplary. But Wigglesworth knew that man never achieves righteousness in this world. He knew that within him lay all the guilt of Adam, and he took pleasure in abasing himself for his sinful heart, for his pride, his over-valuing of creature comforts, his neglect of God. The automatic result of the daily examination of his soul was the conclusion that he was a vile worm, indeed the "chief of sinners."

The modern reader will rightly discount Wigglesworth's claim to preeminence in sin, but his frequent protestations of guilt were more than a pose. Wigglesworth was obsessed with guilt. It is perhaps significant that one of the accusations which he most frequently levelled against himself was a lack of natural affection for his father. At one point he confessed himself secretly glad at his father's death.

We should scarcely exaggerate, I think, if we described Michael Wigglesworth as a morbid, humorless, selfish busybody. In this diary the ugly and somewhat absurd, somewhat pathetic figure of the caricature comes to life, a Roundhead to confirm the last prejudice of the Cavalier. And yet historians have been at some pains to erase this very caricature. The popular picture of the Puritans, it has been shown, is grossly overdrawn, for Puritanism did not exclude the enjoyment of the good things of life. The Puritans read books, wrote verses, and had their pictures painted. They were unashamedly fond of beer and wine and even of more ardent spirits. They liked to eat well and live well and made no pretensions to asceticism. They were not prudish; they made no attempt to stifle natural passions in celibacy. They were men of the world, able to deal equally well with an Indian, a Royalist, or a seidel of beer.

How then are we to interpret Michael Wigglesworth? Was he simply an anomaly, one of those eccentric killjoys who can be found in any society? There are surely good reasons for regarding Wigglesworth as exceptional: he never enjoyed good health, and his bodily weaknesses may have been responsible in large measure for his morbid state of mind; furthermore his preoccupation with his father's death suggests that he may have had some psychological disorder. But to dismiss Wigglesworth as an unhealthy anomaly is to condemn him without a trial. He did, after all, teach at Harvard College; he did serve as minister to a Puritan congregation; and he did write for New England the most popular book of his time. In his own day no one accused him of heresy or eccentricity. Grant that

he was exceptional, which he certainly was, did his singularity con-
stitute a denial, or an intensification, of Puritan values? Was he
exceptionally Puritan or exceptionally unpuritan? Puritanism un-
questionably made rigorous demands on those who subscribed to it.
The fact that Michael Wigglesworth, as revealed in the diary, does
not look like the average New Englander of the seventeenth century
may mean simply that he accepted the demands of Puritanism more
wholeheartedly than most of his countrymen.

To affirm, then, that Wigglesworth was exceptionally and emphatically Puritan is not to cast doubt on what historians have been
saying for the past twenty years, but it is to suggest that the popular
caricature may be closer to the central meaning of Puritanism than
the friends of New England sometimes like to suppose. Although
the popular view fails to do justice to the Puritan; although it
neglects the strength of his conviction, the integrity of his purpose,
and the breadth and subtlety of intellect with which he defended
himself; although it overlooks the fact that he was, after all, a human
being, nevertheless it does emphasize the distinctive features of Puritanism as they now appear to a hedonist world. If the cartoonist
could study and understand Puritanism in all its complexity, he
would probably still draw the same cartoon. For the mark of the
Puritan was not his human warmth but his zeal, his suspicion of
pleasure, his sense of guilt; and it is these qualities which are satirized
in the popular caricature. Michael Wigglesworth, who appears to be
a living embodiment of the caricature, was distinctly and thoroughly
a Puritan. If we measure him by the precepts of the Puritan preachers, it will be apparent, I think, that his sense of guilt, his hostility
to pleasure, even his minding of other people's business, were not
the anomalies of a diseased mind but simply the qualities demanded
of a good Puritan.

To consider the last, most objectionable quality first, did Wigglesworth's concern with other people's sins represent merely the tedious
petulance of a busybody, or was it the expression of some funda-
mental part of Puritan belief? In the light of the social and political
theory expressed by virtually every articulate Puritan, one cannot
escape the conclusion that Puritanism invited, or rather demanded,
active coöperation from every member of society in the eradication
of sin. It was held up as a sign of regeneration that a man should
reform his friends and neighbors. The true convert, Thomas Hooker
explained, was one who sought to destroy all sins. "What ever sins

come within his reach, he labors the removal of them, out of the familyes where he dwels, out of the plantations where he lives, out of the companies and occasions, with whom he hath occasion to meet and meddle at any time."[2] The obligation of the convert to reform those around him was grounded in the covenant by which God sealed the salvation of his elect. "If God make a Covenant, to be a God to thee and thine," John Cotton pointed out, "then it is thy part to see it, that thy children and servants be Gods people." And again, "when we undertake to be obedient to him [God]," we undertake not only "in our owne names, and for our owne parts, but in the behalfe of every soule that belongs to us, . . . our wives, and children, and servants, and kindred, and acquaintance, and all that are under our reach, either by way of subordination, or coördination."[3]

In a place where every serious person was engaged in persuading himself of his own conversion such doctrine was probably sufficient in itself to create a community of busybodies. But the desire to produce evidence of one's own conversion was not the only ground of zeal for the morality of others: The Puritan believed that the outward prosperity of every social group rested upon the prevention of sin among the members. Quite apart from his individual relationship to God through the covenant of grace, every Puritan partook of a more external, social relationship with Him through the societies to which he belonged, through family, church, state, and in Wigglesworth's case, the college. Every social institution existed for the Puritan by virtue of a special covenant with God in which the members had promised obedience to the laws of God.[4] Consequently every Puritan was bound to obey God not merely as a sanctified man (in order to prove to himself that he was saved) but as a member of every group to which he belonged. If he failed, he not only demonstrated his own damnation, but he brought the temporal wrath of God upon his family, upon his church, and upon his state. Thus we find Wigglesworth exclaiming over his sins, "ah Lord! I pul down evils upon others as wel as my self. Sicknesses, death of godly ones, wants, divisions have not my sins a hand in these miserys? oh Lord I am affraid of thy judgements upon my self and others." (p.

[2] Thomas Hooker, *The Application of Redemption* (London, 1659), p. 684.
[3] John Cotton, *The Way of Life* (London, 1641), p. 91; *Christ the Fountaine of Life* (London, 1651), pp. 33-34.
[4] Perry Miller, *The New England Mind. The Seventeenth Century* (New York, 1939), pp. 365-491.

82) These ideas penetrated to every level of society in New England. In 1656, the year in which Wigglesworth accepted a call to preach at Malden, a miserable girl, laboring under the name of Tryal Pore, who had committed the sin of fornication, confessed to the Middlesex County Court that "by this my sinn I haue not only donn what I can to Poull doune Jugmente from the lord on my selue but allso apon the place where I liue."[5]

In view of these beliefs Wigglesworth's zeal for correcting sin is entirely understandable and entirely in accordance with the strictest Puritan doctrine. Since the whole group had promised obedience to God the whole group would suffer at the hands of God for the sins of any delinquent member. Manifestly every member must coöperate in avoiding such a fate. Incessant and universal vigilance was the price of prosperity. It was as if a district occupied by a military force were given notice that for any disorder the whole community— innocent and guilty alike—would be penalized. Every Christian society had received such a notice from God, and its effect upon the godly members, of whom we may account Wigglesworth one, was an extraordinary zeal for bringing others into the paths of righteousness.

A thorough selfishness was by no means inconsistent with this kind of zeal. When the Puritan sought to reform his neighbor, he had no altruistic, humanitarian goal in sight, but simply the fulfillment of his own personal promise to his Creator and the prevention of public calamities in which he himself would be involved. Even Wigglesworth's selfishness in the matter of marriage does not set him off from his contemporaries. All the evidence indicates that marriage in the seventeenth century was a business transaction to which the haggling over dowries and settlements gave more the air of an economic merger than of a psychological union. The Puritans, to be sure, regarded the relationship of husband and wife as one in which love should predominate, but the love was a duty which came after marriage, not a spontaneous passion which preceded it.

In his sense of guilt Wigglesworth likewise exhibited the frame of mind that was expected of a good Puritan. When Anne Hutchinson lost her sense of guilt and declared that God had cast her loose from the bonds of sin, the orthodox members of the Massachusetts government banished her. No one, they felt, could escape from sin

[5] Records of the Middlesex County Court, Cambridge, Mass., folder 28, group 5 (manuscript).

in this world, not even in Massachusetts; and anyone who thought such a thing possible was either insane or in the hands of the devil or both. Thomas Hooker, sometimes considered more liberal than other Puritans, advised his readers that "we must look wisely and steddily upon our distempers, look sin in the face, and discern it to the full." The man who could take such a full view of sin could hardly be a happy human being, for according to Hooker he would be one who

> hath seen what sin is, and what it hath done, how it hath made havock of his peace and comfort, ruinated and laid wast the very Principles of Reason and Nature, and Morality, and made him a terror to himself, when he hath looked over the loathsom abominations that lie in his bosom, that he is afraid to approach the presence of the Lord to bewail his sins, and to crave pardon, lest he should be confounded for them, while he is but confessing of them; afraid and ashamed lest any man living should know but the least part of that which he knows by himself, and could count it happy that himself was not, that the remembrance of of those hideous evils of his might be no more.[6]

Few persons in any time could exhibit a feeling of guilt as strong as that which Hooker here demands. The fact that Wigglesworth did attain something like it is a sign not of eccentricity but of orthodoxy.

If we examine, finally, the sins of which Wigglesworth most often finds himself guilty, we arrive at the origin of Wigglesworth's hostility to pleasure and at the central meaning of Puritanism as Wigglesworth exemplifies it: the belief that fallen man inevitably estimates too highly the creatures and things of this world, including himself. Pride and the overvaluing of "the creature," these are the sins of which Wigglesworth accused himself almost daily, and these are the sins involved in enjoyment of the senses. The Puritan was not exactly hostile to pleasure, but his suspicion was so close to hostility that it often amounted to the same thing. A man might enjoy the things of this world, provided that he did so in proportion to their absolute value, but since their absolute value was insignificant when placed beside the value of their Creator, the amount of pleasure that might lawfully be drawn from them was small indeed. It is not surprising therefore that Wigglesworth seldom recorded specific actions in which he had displayed too high a sense of his own or of the creature's value. The sin did not lie in the action itself, but in the estimate which was placed upon it, as when he found himself too happy with having one of his sermons well received. His sins were sins of attitude, sins of judgment, sins of a will which had been

6 Thomas Hooker, *The Application of Redemption* (London, 1659), pp. 53-54.

debilitated and corrupted by the original fall of man. They were not particular sins but the essence of sin itself. For sin to the Puritan was not simply the breach of a commandment; it was a breach of the order which God had ordained throughout all creation, an order which was inverted by sin and restored by grace. The Puritan God had created the universe to serve His own glory, but He had directed that all parts of that universe, except man, should serve him only indirectly—through serving man. As long as man remained innocent in the Garden of Eden, so long did man enjoy dominion over the creatures and direct communication with his Maker. But sin had inverted the order of things and turned the whole creation topsy-turvy. As one Puritan minister put it, "Man is dethroned, and become a servant and slave to those things that were made to serve him, and he puts those things in his heart, that God hath put under his feet."[7] The only remedy was return to God through Christ, a return which would be completed at the last day and which would be partially consummated here and now through the operation of saving grace. "If sin be (as it is) an aversion or turning away of the soul from God to something else besides him . . . then in the work of grace there is a conversion and turning of the soul towards God again, as to the best and cheifest good of all."[8] Again and again Puritan ministers warned their listeners that "the onely sutable adequate ultimate object of the soul of man is god himselfe," that "all true christians have Christ as the scope and End of their lives," that "no creature that is finite, can be the end of the Soul nor give satisfaction to it."[9] Thus, in recognizing that he placed too high a value on the creatures, Wigglesworth was recognizing that in him the divine order was still inverted. No matter how often he told himself that God was the supreme good to which all else must be subordinated, no matter how loudly he called upon God to make him believe, he could not help overestimating himself and the world.

In this undeviating scrutiny of his own corruption Wigglesworth was probably not a typical Puritan, as he was not a typical human being; but he was closer to the ideals of Puritanism than were his more warm-blooded contemporaries who indulged the flesh and enjoyed the creatures. In the pages that follow he has left the record of a mind which had the strength to digest what seems to us a bitter

[7] Urian Oakes, *A Seasonable Discourse* (Cambridge, Mass., 1682), p. 27.

[8] Richard Mather, *Farewell Exhortation* (Cambridge, Mass., 1657), p. 20.

[9] From John Hull's manuscript notes of sermons in the library of the Massachusetts Historical Society.

doctrine. The document has none of the chatty gossip that has made Samuel Sewall's work so widely known, nor does it have the effusive facility of Cotton Mather's diary. Wigglesworth's meditations are neither pretty nor pleasant, but they are, I think, emphatically, uniquely Puritan.

The Manuscript

The diary of Michael Wigglesworth has been transcribed from the original manuscript in the library of the Massachusetts Historical Society and is here printed with the kind permission of that society and of The Colonial Society of Massachusetts, in the pages of whose *Publications* (Volume XXXV, pages 311-444) it first appeared.

The manuscript is a small bound volume containing 160 un-numbered pages. The first 132 pages (pages 3 to 100 of the present edition) are a personal record kept by Wigglesworth from February, 1653, to May, 1657. For the first fourteen months the record has been kept fairly regularly from day to day or at least from week to week, but subsequent entries are spasmodic, with numerous gaps of several months each. At page 132 (page 100 of this edition) the record ends; the writing at the bottom of this page is inverted and is the last of a number of entries which begin at the other end of the volume. These entries are miscellaneous in character, consisting prin-cipally of declarations of religious experience, apparently made be-fore the congregation of Wigglesworth's church by persons apply-ing for admission. In the present edition this second part of the volume has been printed continuously with the first, so that page 100 corresponds with the first page at the back of the manuscript.

Although the greater part of the volume is written in longhand, there are numerous passages, varying in length from a single word to several pages, of shorthand code. In the diary proper the longest of these passages is less than a page, but in the second part all the statements of religious experience have been recorded in shorthand. The code which Wigglesworth used was that of Thomas Shelton,[10] a rather complex system, which provided separate characters for all the letters of the alphabet (though vowels were usually indicated by

[10] *Tachygraphy. The Most exact and compendious methode of short and swift writing that hath euer yet beene published by any. Composed by Thomas Shelton. Author and professor of the said Art. Approued by both Vniuersities.* London. Printed for Samuel Cartwright, 1641.

the positions of consonants), for the principal syllables, and for 268 common words. In this multitude of symbols, many resembling each other, the meaning of any character depended much upon the context in which it appeared. Even at best the code is difficult to decipher, but Wigglesworth further complicated it by introducing many original characters of his own. Consequently in a number of places, six in all, the manuscript has proved undecipherable. None of these places, however, contains more than a few words.

Except in these few undecipherable areas shorthand passages have been expanded and written in modern English spelling. The original punctuation, which is indicated in the code by special symbols, has been preserved, and in the longhand passages both the original punctuation and the original orthography, excluding abbreviations, have been retained. Abbreviations have been expanded, except in the case of words which are normally abbreviated today and in cases where the word abbreviated is doubtful. Where punctuation is missing but obviously needed, the end of a sentence has been indicated by a blank space of three ems. Shorthand has been indicated by italics.

My initial preparation of the manuscript for the press was greatly facilitated by a grant from the Colonial Society of Massachusetts.

E. S. M.

THE DIARY OF
MICHAEL WIGGLESWORTH
1653-1657

THE TEXT

If the unloving carriages of my pupils can goe so to my heart as they doe; how then doe my vain thoughts, my detestable pride, my *unnatural filthy lust that are so oft and even this day in some measure stirring in me* how do these griev my lord Jesus that loves me infinitely more then I do them? Do I take it heavily that my love is so lightly made of? ah! lord Jesus how fearful is my despizing of thy dying love, of thy love in giving me thy self after thou seemedst to haue cast me of for ever? ah! I cannot love thee, not fear to sin against thee, although thou exercise me with such crosses, as again this day, wherein I may read my owne ill carriages toward thee. And dost thou yet make any beam of thy love break out toward me, after any fears? Nay have so oft and so long comforted my self with thy love amidst my daily sins. The enmity and contrariety of my heart to seeking thee in earnest, with my want of dear affection to thee, these make me affraid. but thou did giue me thy self in the Lords supper, thou dist giue me a heart (though vile) to lay hold of the desiring all from thee. and this giues me hope. blessed be thy name.

Pride and vain thoughts again prevail over me to the grief of my god. clense me, o lord, when shall it once be? I had opportunity (purposely takeing of it) to discourse with one of my pupils much of the things of god; as also with another out of the colledge whom I went to visit, who spake something to me about his spiritual condition, the lord helping me to speak much to him again with some affection: the Lord bless it to them both. *My pupil was John Haines.*[1] *I spoke to them both what a blessed thing it was to serve and seek the Lord.*

peevishness vain thoughts and especially pride still prevails in me. I cannot think one good thought, I cannot do any thing for god but presently pride gets hould of me. but I feel a need of christ's blood to wash me from the sins of my best dutys and from all that deadness of heart, and want of spirit for god this day. I find my heart prone to take secret pleasure in thinking how much I do for others' good: but Lord how little of it is done for the. I fear there is much sensuality and doting upon the creature in my pursuit of the good of others; I cannot seek gods glory therein but am carry'd most with pitty to man. else the Lord would hardly cross me in my endeavours and hopes: were it not to shew me, that both my labours and those persons whom I haue greatest hopes of are also vanity. Lord why is my soul glutted

7th

[1] John Haynes, son of Governor John Haynes, graduated from Harvard in 1656 and returned to England, where in 1668 he became rector of the church at Swansey in Essex.

so with my owne projects that I oft times feel little need of thy self *Small cause then to be proud of the love I bear to these which thou hast given me when by love to them I cease loving of thee.* Lord heal this wound this day.

Sabbath 13 This Sabbath I found both my naturall strength and spirits somewhat low, and my spiritual affections very dead. Both in the forenoon and after I found remarkable experiments of my owne blindness when god withdrawes: being not able to understand some truths delivered especially afternoon I was almost quite nonplus't about the trinity but beseeching the lord to open mine ey's I soon saw in some measure the truth both before noon, and afterward at which I stuck before. And here god heard my prayer. Innumerable vain thoughts crowded in upon me this day, and I find it utterly impossible to overcome them my self, I cannot for my life withdraw my mind from an unsutable object it is so forced upon me: but ah! I am oft slouthful and lay down the weapons of my warfare and do not fight, cry strive as I should against them. the dispensation of so waighty a truth as that, he that beleiv's not is condemn'd already seem'd to me too scholastically exprest and not with vehemency sufficiently prest, so that I could not but undervalue. At noon I found fretting prevail over me, though upon gods day that others could not understand my words: although my lord bear with my dulness, and take pains himself to teach me. o for this I desire to hang down my head with shame before god. I neglected also to speak to some whom I heard profanely laughing aloud Lord forgiue this neglect.

14 (2d) Now that I am to goe out into the world I am affraid, nay I know I shall lose my heart and my affections, I can do nothing for god receiv nothing from him but tis a snare unto me. why Lord thou art the guide of my youth into thy hands I commit my spirit, thou art my whole trust giue me to make the soe continually, let me walk in the light of thy countenance all the day long catervatim opprimer iniquitatum multitudinibus ipsiss. hoc die.

15 Pride I feel still again and again abounding, self-admiration, though destroying my self daly. god gracious and bountifull in bestowing in directing me and mine, but I unthankfully wickedly making gods gifts subservient to my vain glory. ah Lord I am vile, I desire to abhor my self (o that I could!) before the for these things. *I find such unresistable torments of carnal lusts or provocation unto the ejection of seed that I find my self unable to read any thing to inform me about my distemper because of the prevailing or rising of my lusts. This I have procured to my self. God hath brought this to my eye this day Thou hast destroyed thy self but in me is thy help Lord let me find help in thee though I have destroyed my self by my iniquity*

4th day. 3 speciall times pride remarkably prevailing in me.   besides   16
passionate distempers inwardly prevail.   vain thoughts *carnal lusts some also*.
I feel my self unable to beat into my heart any great affection of sorrow or
shame for my pride: ah Lord harden not my heart from thy fear. oh lift
up the light of thy countenance upon me, for in thy favour is my life.

I took a good deal of time this day to look thorowly into the vilenes of   17
that sin of pride. And see that which might make me go mourning all my
dayes, yet I can find little heart breaking for it, nor power against it. I
found my spirit in a troubled perplexed sunken frame this day, propense to
fretting: yet so sensual and mind so full of vain thoughts, as I could not
get my heart into a praying frame. a little at length the Lord did breath
this evening, and giues me to see, the riches of his love continued, though I
continue my provocations. And oh that I could se still more of my owne
vileness, and the sweet louve of my gracious god, whom woe is me I abuse.

*The last night a filthy dream and so pollution escaped me in my sleep for which
I desire to hang down my head with shame and beseech the Lord not to make me
possess the sin of my youth and give me into the hands of my abomination.* I find both
pride in speciall so monstrous prevalent again and again this day, and vain
thoughts together with wearines of the length of dutys in the morning, also sensuall outgoings of heart or proneness thereto, and so to crossness and
peevishness, slighting of others, lashing out in too much eagerness of spirit
in discours, dishonouring god and shaming my self thereby; in a word my
heart and words and actions go wholy out of frame, and voyd of any thing
of god, that I see my sin is aboue measure sinfull; I loath my self, and could
even take vengeance of my self for these abominations. yet I feel, a stone
in my heart that knows not how to melt. but I fly to a mediator laden with
sin, oh Lord make it a hevier load to me. I despair of ever pleasing god by
my endeavours in the world: my whole hopes are in thee for pardon, for
power according to thy promiss. I am thine, I seek thee I trust in thee, suffer not mine enemies, thine enemies to triumph over me.

*I had some burden upon my spirit and was in some measure laden with my sins
before meeting but this is my misery I find that at the Public Assembly when attending upon God where I should get the greatest good my sense of my sin and
misery is most worn away so that its with me as with him at the pool when I am
come thither why I have none to put me in nay I lose my sense of my need of going
in. Vain thoughts and pride at noon pride at night* cause me to loath and abhor my
self   Behold I am vile behold I am vile *what shall I say* to the o preserver of
men   why hidest thou thy face from me, why dost thou let lose my sins
upon me? I would mourn but cannot, I would forsake them and overcom
them but cannot. Lord saue me, I am thine. a dead proud, froward,

filthy heart make me an abhorrence to my god and a burden to my self. Lord for thy Covenant sake eas me of this body of death.

on the 2d *day* vain thoughts in holy dutys principally molested me. vexation and rebuke the Lord still increaseth and casts shame upon me, by suffering some of mine to bring shame upon the society;[2] or at least to divulge our shame. *Also pride prevailed and that to the speaking somewhat too slightly on the President's going against the fellows in John Stone's business.[3] For both which I desire to be humbled*

On the 3d day prevailed in me pride vain thoughts and inordinate outgoing of my spirit in pleading about things like to come and at a great distance. Some what of that spirit came in delightedness of old to feed my self with vain fantasms of things never like to be from which Lord deliver me.

Pride exceeding prevailed on the 4th day. And also too much going out of the heart in hopes on curing the distemper of body by the use of some contrived means. Want of love to God and delight in God. I haue found more sensible weakness of body and pressure by the spleen and flatulent humours this week than for so oft together this winter before. god still crosses outwardly, and I meet with vexation and rebuke. yet pride and vain thoughts are too hard for me, and I find my self too weak to make resistance. ah! Lord hast to my help: be thou my defence and the stay of my soul, for all others fail me. why art thou as a man astonisht that cannot saue? make thy face shine upon me; so shall I rejoyce in thy saluation. teach me thy way's (for I see my blindness) thou wilt lead the blind in a way they haue not knowne.

(Feb. 25
26

6./7)

Deal not with me according to the pride this day exceedingly again prevailing over me. *Some filthiness escaped me in a filthy dream. The Lord notwithstanding.* the lord notwithstanding. enlarged my heart in prayer in the morning in private; and again breathed some sweet affection into my heart in reading of his word at night also spake to my personall sins in Exposition in the hall. Let not your heart be troubled. &c. I find that when things go cross with me, then am I sunken in spirit and disquieted. when I haue hopes of doing or obtaining good, my affections are taken up with that, so that it is very hard for me to set my heart upon god himself and not to rest in the creature, or else to be restless and disconsolate: although I see god is as willing to haue me come into his presence, and to satisfy my soul in sweet communion with himself, and infinitely more willing, than I am that any of them I loue most should be near me, and that I could be

[2] By "the society" Wigglesworth probably means Harvard College.
[3] John Stone, possibly the son of the Reverend Samuel Stone of Hartford, graduated from Harvard in 1653 and shortly thereafter returned to England.

communicating the greatest good unto them, which certainly is one of the main things I desire upon earth at present: the want of this on their part griues me, and vexeth me daly. how then do I grieue the spirit of my god, in that I will not come to him, who desires to giue me life? who is therefore forced to vex and trouble me in the creature, to make me seek joy and comfort in himself. Ah foolish wretch that wilt be placing thy hope where thou hast so oft seen 'tis not to be had! ah sensuall spirit, that art so avers from savouring the things of god, his grace his will, his ordinances,! that cannot feed upon the heavenly manna and be satisfy'd, but when creatures fail thy heart fail's: when creatures smile god is undervalew'd. teach me at length, o Lord, to feel a continually [*sic*] necessity of god in christ. deliver me from pride, my cruel taskmaster thou hast giv'n me some comfort in beleiving this week, from that ground because thou hast made thy word efficacious to me given me an effectuall call a personal call, a clear call taking away all my objections, and bringing up my spirit to gospel termes: assure this to me yet more, enlarg my desires after it.

I am affraid of those vile frames of my heart viz. a carnall spirit that cannot relish and savour the things of god that can feed upon my owne hopes or endeavours, letting god and christ ly by and not make christ my life. also of slouth that cannot away with the paines required in dutys, in warring against sin. this makes me sometimes weary of divine services: sometimes neglectiue of my spirituall war against sin. Lord I am now going to the pool o do thou put me in and heal me. Lord remove my unbeleif which makes that I cannot Expect redemption from my prevailing corruptions in this world: and that I think is one thing that makes me more earnest for others than for my self because I can beleiv god is willing to justify, but cannot see that he is as ready to sanctify

I found god in the forenoon mightily affecting my heart in publick prayer in the assembly: also awakning my heart and stirring up fear within me. Mr. Dunster[4] preaching to the purpose that when god hides his face and melts a people for their sins why they are left helpless and heartless under his hand. out of 64 Isaiah 7. After noon god pleased to giue some affection and to warm my heart a little with the loue and grace of christ coming and dwelling amongst us. yet in the fore part of the sermon I found my spirit so distracted *with* vain thoughts and so disquieted within me, because one of my pupils was ill and absent from the ordinances, that I could not attend to the word, I could not cry for help scarcely to heaven nor see the evill of those impatient disquietments yet I desir'd a heart to

---

[4] Henry Dunster was president of Harvard from 1640 to 1654. He was forced to resign when he abandoned the orthodox Congregational belief in infant baptism.

cry for help, and the lord set me free at length from them. yet sundry times this day pride prevald over me. And some fears because I feel not loue to god as I should, but more loue to man, least I should loue man more than god. I am laden with a body of death, and could almost be willing to be dissolved and be with christ free'd from this sinful flesh, saue that I fear my state and haue some misgiuings; yet I desire to be made sincere, what is amis lord amend! assure me of thy loue that I may be prepared for life or death

2d/28   Again I find my spirit disrested, and my studys my spirit finds somewhat sapless; I would now take up my rest in god, yet cannot assure my heart of his love, so as to be prepar'd to dy the lord onely can speak it to my heart, and deliver me from that sensuality (that can overrelish the creature, but not tast sweetness in god) from that pride, and those vain thoughts which all this day prevail in me. Lord suffer not thy poor prisoner to perish by the Corruptions which I see and cry out against which I would hate and loath more, but cannot.

Annus Novus
1653

March//

1   this morning god let in some comfortable perswasion of his love to me. yet after vain thoughts prevail'd in holy dutys: and Pride in all my actions. shame devours all my labours, in stead of admiring god I admire my self. for this I loath my self. And I am affraid of that deadness of affection to godward, and those loose straglings of my soul unto other things, so that I haue not power to relish the things of god, not power to cry to him. out of a deep dungeon father I groan to the of this cursed, feared malady. let it not be in vain that I desire help, and would cry but cannot.

2   This day was brought news of that dreadful disaster at Boston by fire;[5] which came to pass the very night before Mr. Mitchels[6] lecture concerning god['s] judgements, and how abused they aggravate sin. thus god seals his word with his dreadful works. my heart was much affected and dejected within me upon deep thoughts of these things and what I had heard god speak to me in his word, (for he met with sundry of my sins and gaue

[5] The fire destroyed eight houses and was afterward known as "the great fire" until the fire of 1676 superseded it for that distinction. See the letter of John Endecott to John Winthrop, Jr., in Massachusetts Historical Society *Collections*, 4th series, VI, 155.

[6] Jonathan Mitchel graduated from Harvard in 1647 and three years later succeeded Thomas Shepard as pastor of the church in Cambridge.

dreadful examples of gods judgments that should haue warned me from them) yet affterward, o amazing prodigious, overpowering prevalency of wickedness,! pride again, and again most fearfully after all those shakings, awaknings, and almost sinkings of spirit, discovered its power over me. ah Lord! my king, my god, thee thee I provoke, and wert thou not a god indeed, infinite in thy grace fire and brimstone, or a flood of wrath had seized on me long ere now. why hast thou not pluck't away from me by some sad stroke my dearest ones? am I better, nay how far am I viler than they to whom thou hast done this. my want of watchfulness against or my bouldness to vain thought I am affraid of. I haue sin'd I fear in the Salem business, against god and man, in not coming clear with Cambridge first, in saying I was not ingaged to any others.[7] I haue sin'd also in not being serious enough in prayer to god for guidance in it, untill I now be call'd to Boston about it. god may justly leav me, and put me to shame for my sin, and not pitty me because I find both to day and formerly a spirit that cannot sutably pitty others in misery.

I still find abundance of pride, and more regarding what man thinks of /5
me than what gods thoughts are of me. And much distracted thoughts I find arising from too much doting affection *to some of my pupils one of whom went to Boston with me today.* I feel no power to love and prize god in my heart, my spirit is so leavend with love to the creature. this frame I am affraid of, this I desire to mourn under. yet god leavs me not without some shakings and visitations of his spirit in his ordinances this day Mr. Sherman[8] preaching at Boston upon that, quench not the spirit. I desire to make god my rest when creatures I see fail. I desire to be asham'd that I thus requite the lord to dispize him who dispizeth not me but comforts me, when all comforters for sake me.

Pride principally prevailing   6.

Vain thoughts in holy dutys, peevishness of spirit against man, and im-   7.
patience towards god, in reference to my pupils, finding all my pains so fruitless for their spirituall good, disquietment of spirit hereupon ariseth; and my vile heart would rather stay and comfort itself with projecting other means for the future, than betake it self to god for the present. Lord pardon, Lord heal these distempers. Lord shed thy love abroad in my heart, inflame me with loue to thee again, giving hope and assurance in beleeving, and patience in waiting thy pleasure for doing good either to me or

---

[7] At this time Wigglesworth was preparing to assume the ministry of a church. Apparently he had considered a proposal from the Salem church at the same time that he was negotiating with the church in Cambridge.

[8] John Sherman, educated at Cambridge University, came to New England in 1634 and in 1647 became minister of Watertown.

mine. harden not my heart from thy fear and love. I am affraid because
I feel so little love to the. where are those sweet breathings of thy spirit
which some times I haue found. O restore to me the sence of thy favour
which is better than life. Let me see my endeavours in my place accepted
of thee in Christ Jesus, though I cannot yet see any comfortable effect they
produce. in the Lord Jesus alone I present them to thee. and my self to
thee in this thy approaching sabboth.

1   Mr. Mitchel preacht twice to day upon 1 John. 14 and we saw his glory.
Now woe is me! that I cannot see christs glory, I never find my heart
more carnall, and my eys more blind that I cannot behold and feel a present excellency in christ, than when his glory is display'd before me. my
love to christ is gone and all savour of his sweetness in a manner, so that I
may with trembling fear the vileness of my owne heart, when christ is
most to be seen. ah Lord my rock, and my fortress whose glory I have
seen, who hast bin my stay when other things failed: blind not my eys,
withold not the outshinings of thy favour, the creatures do fail, o why
cannot I feel that satisfaction in thy self that sometimes I haue found? why
hides thou thy sweet face, and witholdest thy spirit of supplication also,
that I cannot mightily cry after thee. Verily thou art my father: though
my spot be not the spot of thy children, witness my dayly sensuall glutting
my heart with creature comforts, witness this days pride and vain thoughts
that overrun my soul (I am not able to think a thought aright) yet art thou
my father, thou hast found me when lost, comforted me when destressed,
assisted me when unable to do thy will, thy visitations preserv my daly decaying spirits, thy right hand upholds me. why restore to me the joy of thy
salvation; caus thy face to shine upon me and I shall be saved. Put the
spirit of a child into me and constantly maintain it, for I fade as a leaff and
my iniquitys like the wind take me away.

*Vain thoughts break in upon me. My soul cant get over a disconsolate troubled
devoted frame in reference to my pupils and other troubles concerning Ah Lord
let me see thy face that will fill up all my emptiness and the dissatisfaction I
find in the creature. I wait and oh that I could long for thy salvation O where
are thy tender compassions and bowel mercies which I have been comforted with
when low O hide not thy face from me O thou that hath delivered my feet out
of the miry clay O thou that hath brought me out of the iron furnace to whom I
have sung songs of praise.*

3d. 4/   *O wretch that I am my iniquity like clay and fetters holds me down that the
good I would do I cant the evil I would not do that do I. Nay I feel my heart apt
secretly to give way to my vain thoughts in holy duties and glued as it were to my
sensuality or love to the creature full of hope since and cant get over sinking and dis-*

quietments of spirit (because things go not well with my pupils) and as for pride why it overcomes me in holiest duties where there should be most abasement   The Lord has given me several opportunities of grace more than ordinary this week as one lecture and two private meetings but my heart at both was so vile that I may even be a burden to my self.

Very much pride yet prevailes, and hypocrisy: my bodily strength ffails me so that I can scarce do any thing, but in assaying am a weariness to my self.   my sins are too hard for me: my desires in reference to my journey[9] are crost: expectations fail   all is vanity.   why Lord withold not now thy grace and good spirit, giving patience under thy hand, that I may be willing to miss this opportunity and still to bear my infirmitys, till thy time come when thou wilt commaund health.   o assure me of thy love, and then I know all shall work for my good. 5th/

These petitions the Lord heard in part, giving me some measure of content to goe or stay. And after all this he graciously prosper'd me, I still continuing my endeavours after a horse. Some comfort god gaue me in himself finding my love to man not rewarded with like love again: he helpt me to rejoyce in the testimony of a good conscience, and looking to him not to man for reward of my labours.   he kept my heart this day somewhat nearer to him than ordinary.   yet both this day pride, and the next day pride and vain distracting thoughts molested me in holy duty's. *I find my spirit so exceeding carried with love to my pupils that I cant tell how to take up my rest in God   Lord for this cause I am afraid of my wicked heart   Fear takes hold of me. God assisted me so to speak to my pupils this day that I could hardly utter my self without pouring forth tears though notwithstanding I desire to look up to the Lord and wait his time for a blessing upon it and in the mean time oh make thy face shine upon me and be thou my saviour   Suffer me not suffer me not O my God to dote upon the creature wherein is nothing but vanity and vexation of spirit. Show me thy glory O my God*

Mr. Dunster preacht today about the thorny ground.   god was pleased to set in and awaken my heart, and fear seiz'd upon me because I found that the cares I had for the good of others, and my affection to them, and my selfseeking therein, had got into my heart and drunk up my very spirit and stoln my heart from god: and these thorns do overshadow the seed of the word so that I cannot see the glory of god and christ, by reason of seeming excellency in these things. But upon search I find, that though thorns do thus grow, yet I disallow them, and would fain pull them, but cannot, I do resist them and strive to take up satisfaction in god, though I find little. I find god has bin my daly rest (as it were) in whose bosom

[9] A journey to New Haven (see p. 12).

alone I haue found repose when forlorn of the creature. In the Afternoon. I heard 22 ezra 2 ult. Marks to examin by whether we make breaches, or make them up. Concerning some of them I haue the testimony of a good conscience bearing witness for me: that I most fear that I haue lost my first love, which thinge provokes god to come against the place where I liue as a theef in the night.

Innumerable evils compass me about, and prevail against me, wherefore I am affraid and asham'd and unable to see god still loving me with an everlasting love. I find so much of my spirit goe out unto the creature, unto mirth, that there is little savour of god left in my soul. the creature and thoughts and cares about it get so into my heart, that I cannot get my thoughts free for god in prayer in the hall. much impatient disquietments do (will I nil I) get mastery over me having sent to Boston this morning timely, and hearing no answer before night. God crosses me in very faithfulness to meeken me and teach me submit to his will, and let out less affection unto what I haue in hand, for which I magnify his name; yet I am affraid of my own vileness: vain words also or jesting I fear my self guilty of. oh who know's the errour of his wayes. yet Lord pardon, for christ's sake and return refresh my soul with thy loving kindness early. so shall I know that thou even thou onely art god and good, and that there none besides thee.

March the 23 I came to New Haven being upon my journey from tuesday after noon to Dedham, unto Wednesday the next week at night. I preacht my first sermon at Pequit[10] by the way 32 Deuteronomy 9./ Much difficulty I found in my journey, my back and brest almost shak't in pieces with riding. in my pain and anguish I lift up my heart and voyce to the lord my god, and he helpt me through the difficulty, giuing me so much strength as enabled me to bear it. We were lost the first day and rode above an hour within evening: god brought us to a house where we had a guid to our desired place. near pequit we were lost and past through craggy dangerous way yet god kept us and all [that] belonged to us; and brought us safe notwithstanding the rumours of the Indian plots.

this sabbath I found much inlargement in private dutys, yet pride thereupon prevailing, which I desir'd to resist and loath my self for. I find vain thoughts and a vile heart ready to giue them lodging, slow to se and feel any evil in them. a slouthful frame that cannot away with taking pains in seeking god in resisting sin, but ready to giue way to it. And there is also a carnal heart that cannot savour the things of god, but whoarishly departs from him. what impressions and tasts of himself god leavs at present are

[10] New London.

soon gone: this makes me exceedingly affraid of my self and my owne spirit of whoardoms. these things open a gap to unbeleif; I am ashamed to lift up mine eys to heaven and call god my gracious father, my onely portion, seing I deal so unworthyly with him; in my trouble saying arise and save me; noe sooner deliver'd but lightly esteeming the rock of my salvation; soe deaded in my affections toward him, that when I come nearest to him in publick ordinances, then is my heart apt to be furthest from him thus am I chaned down under my boults and fetters, and cannot so much as lift up one living desire toward god at some times: if at any time I do why how soon vanish they? thou hidest thy face Lord; and I am troubled, my soul is troubled within me. thou witholdest thy spirit and my strength is gone, I haue no might but become even as another man. weak as water. Lord I haue no might nor strength, thou art my hope, be thou my helper, who never faylest them who trust in the. I am unworthy of mercy, let that ashame me. thou art worthy to bestow mercy let that incourage me. I beleiv Lord help my unbeleif which is great; there is help with thee for un-beleif for the most devilish distempers as I heard this day out of matthew 17.14. 15. 16. 17 &c. Lord I am thine, save me. I am asham'd that I walk as if I were not thine. pardon me in the blood of the everlasting Covenant.

Grievous fears were again stirring in my [*sic*] and disquieting my heart upon that awaking lecture sermon calling upon us to awake from sleep and stand up from the dead, from dead works.

On thursday morning the Lord was pleas'd to give me somewhat a heart-breaking meditation of him. so that I thought and will the Lord now again return and embrace me in the arms of his dearest love? wil he fall upon my neck and kiss me? for he was pleased to giue in some secret and silent evidence of his love.

But ah wretched backsliding heart! what evil hast thou found in god that thy love and affection to him are so quickly could? that thou secretly departest from him not savouring the things of god, going awhoaring in thy desires after vanity's, seeking thy self, like an empty vine bringing forth fruit to thy self? I abhor my self before the Lord for my shameless pride, especially now when god is abasing me. I am ashamed of my apostatiz-ing heart of unbeleef in departing from the living god, to whom in my dis-tress I am ever crying arise and saue me: I am affraid of my want of nat-ural affection and pitty to my afflicted parents.

Mr. Hook[11] preaching out of 3 Jeremiah 22. 23 Return ye backslid-ing children &c. Lord I see I am a grievous backslider daly revolting from

---

[11] William Hooke preached at New Haven from 1644 to 1656, at which time he returned to England and became a domestic chaplain to Cromwell.

thee in heart and life, going awhoaring loosing my first loue; insomuch that I cannot at some times I cannot gasp and pant after the communications of thy departing spirit.   why I ly down in my shame, before thee   if thou wilt return no more, why 'tis but what I deserv; yet Let me plead with the for thy owne name. *Hast thou not led me with thine everlasting love and therefore drawn me   Can thy love be changed   Can my sin make the faith of God of none effect.*   dost thou not say return and I will heal your backsliding   why I come unto thee   thou art the Lord my god.   in vain seek I comfort elsewhere   O let me *find* it in thy self.

I think I never had my folly so uncased, as since my coming home, both in my indiscretion in taking on me so perplexed and chargeable a journey, in every point whereof much rash inconsiderateness and resolvedness upon it though to great disadvantage appears. And in sundry other respects god makes my father an instrument of so discovering my weak and silly management of every business, that he makes my savour to stink in my owne nosethrils.   this he did most eminently this week immediately after a proud fit of my owne. God abaseth the proud! My heart as 'tis asham'd of my self so it swells against my father, and cannot conceiv such things to proceed from loue, because that covers a multitude of infirmitys, but this rakes them open to the bottom.   but whether he be to blame or no; surely I am, in causing such things and in looking so much at man in the reproving them with discontent. I know my self guilty in the former   I suspect my self in the latter   Lord pardon both, heal both for thy mercy sake. I am affraid of my secret whorish outgoings of spirit after future contrivances, and that my heart bears up it self so much on them. I condemn my self for deadness and hypocrisy and weariness in holy dutys.   father condemn not thou me, but forgiue, and heal my backslidings.   renew a right spirit within me. Asher shall not saue me.   men and creatures present or hoped for cannot, shall not satisfy me and feed my soul.   o do thou communicate thy sweet self who hast made me more glad than the wicked when their corn and oil increaseth. Where are those sure abiding mercy's of david?   those pleasures at thy right hand for ever more?   o hide not thy face from me! Withold not thy good spirit though I deserve it.   heal my languishing soul pitty and cure my frail body. I cannot muse of thee and mourn after the as I should do without overthrowing my bodily health.   thou commands me for health sake to be cheerful.   lift up the light of thy countenance, that I may have cause to be so: season me with the savour of thy spirit that I may not grow loose and licentious hereupon.   fit me for, and bless to me thy approaching sabbath.

I was somewhat dejected with some feares in the forenoon and was not got clear of them in the evening of the sabbath, having heard Mr. Davenport[12] preach how and what a winter christians indeed might goe through both in respect of grace and comfort. my daly decayes of love to god and savour of the things of god, this prophane loos heart that is weary of watchful attending upon god in holy dutys fills me with fears of my owne estate. chewing upon such cogitations I thought that if god would not saue me at last, yet there was something that pleased me in this, that my Lord should haue glory in my damnation: Hereupon I reflected upon my self, saying and whence hast thou any such indearedness of affection to christs glory? can thou desire his glory without some dram of love to him? canst thou love him except he loved the first? then has god indeed loved the with an everlasting love? this somewhat reviued me. I further mused: Can the hypocrite delight himself in the Almighty as I have bin (through mercy) inabled to do when all other helps and hopes haue fayled me? the scripture propounds the querie, as who should say he cannot. yea but I cannot at the present find that heart peace which sometimes I haue done in god. my hopes and expectations quite fail in the creature; my heart is bent to seek it in new contrivances, but I know they are vanity; and I would seek it in god, but I cannot find it there: nay I am weary soon of attending upon god in prayer and meditation that I might find it: this makes me affraid of my owne vile heart, and that enmity against God: off that daly pride which I find again and again prevailing, and common unsavoury spirit. but Lord my god my King, my father I haue put my trust in thee to change my vile heart and in thee I will yet trust, I am vile and fals-hearted, o that I could mourn for't! thou art faithfull and true, thy mercys inhaustible, everlasting. for thy name sake come in and giue me some sweet soul ravishing communion with thy self, that I may know 'tis not a vain thing to seek thee; Let thy visitation preserve my decaying spirit.

The Lord was pleased very particularly to speak unto me and my condition on the last lecture day by Mister Davenport. Concerning my finding my spirit then most content from God and dead when I should draw most near to him. His counsel was then to cry to the Lord Jesus for help for some leastwise gave up most through want of spiritual watch.

On the fast day Mr. D out of 55 Isaiah 6. shewd how the prayer of fayth seeks god himself more than any particular good from god. being conscious to my self how little I could desire god himself and further communion

---

[12] John Davenport was one of the founders of the New Haven Colony and pastor of the church there until 1667. In that year he accepted a call to the First Church at Boston in circumstances that occasioned a schism in the First Church and the founding of the Third Church.

with him than I had attain'd, nay that I haue oft such fits of prophaness that I can se little or no bewty in god and communion with him, nor so much as cry to heaven against that plague: my soul was exceedingly affraid and brought to the dust before god, and great doubtings of my estate both yesterday morning and again today morning. but it pleas'd god in some measure to scatter them: when I consider how god did clearly once and again draw me to his son for all good though I could find none in my self: then making with me a Covenant wel ordred in all things and sure, which therefore remayns though I cannot find such sensible qualifications in my self: which I desire bitterly to bewayl before god, yet whilest I liue I will not let him goe. But moreover I appeal to god himself the searcher of hearts to see whether, there be or haue been no prizing god aboue other things. what then means my restlessness after sin committed untill I haue made my peace with god: or if that be from fear of punishment rather than loue to thy self Lord, yet what meanes that substantial soul-content that I haue found in thy self when creatures haue fayled, and which I never found any where but in thy self. what means that assurance upon this ground given me at Harford, the same being again and again sensibly experienced at Cambridge before my admission into the church? what is that gives me support when creatures frown? is it not thy smiles? when I cannot receiv what I desire from thee is it not that I haue all in thee, and that thou art mine who art better than all? Away then unbeleef and soul-sinking discouragements. I cannot maintain indeed my prizing thee as I should, my seeking after thee as I would. but this prophane heart of mine and my proud heart, are they not my plague thou knowest they are a terrour to me, and make me so to my self. And wilt not thou deliver from this plague when I cry? why Lord remember thy Covenant to redeem me from all iniquity, and hear my prayer, the prayer of thy poor prisoner, and answer my request which is according to thy will. Caus thy face to shine upon me for the Lords sake. *I sought the Lord also this day for health that I may be able to glorify him in my place and so for guiding me in point of settlement.*[13] *I shall wait what God the Lord shall speak in answer to my cry*

On the 6t day which was the next day after the fast: God let me se the prevalency of a multitude of abominable sins in me. As 1: wearinèss of Gods service; in which is great unbelief, though god haue said 'tis not a vain thing to seek him: great unthankfulness for such a gracious opportunity which the damned would prize at a high rate: great slouthfulness that cannot away with taking pains in constant seeking god vizt spirituall worship. 2. peevishness and impaciency, though god were patient and bore long my

[13] Settlement as minister of a church.

dulness nay aversness to learn of him now groundless anger makes me giue place to the Devil so that my spot is not the spot of Gods children: 3. Affirming that for truth which I doubt or am not certain of; now who is the father of lies? 4. want of natural affection to my father, in desiring the continuance of his life *which God ranks among those sins whereto men were given up of God to a reprobate mind.* Lord why hast thou caus'd me to er from thy wayes, or hardened my heart from thy fear? 5. *Want of honoring my mother yea slighting of her speech now the eye that despises his mother the ravens of the valley shall peck it out and the young ravens shall eat it. Lord I cant stand before thee because of these abominations. Against thee I have committed them not obeying thy holy rules though thou didst redeem me for thy self to thy service. Nay 6ly I find again whorish desertions of my heart from God to the creature.* it pleas'd god to make me earnest in prayer both that evening and the next morning for pardon of them for Jesus his sake and for power against them according to gods Covenant to redeem me from all iniquity. *Christ came to redeem poor prisoners* Lord I am prisoner to my sins, chain'd down by them so that I cannot lift my feet to thy testimonies cannot prize the and communion with thee. but what I do I allow not. 'tis sin in me therefore, not I. deliver me from this body of death for I betake me to the onely: and such as come to the thou wilt not cast off. such as labour and are heavy laden thou wilt eas.

The Lord is very urgent with backsliders to return (out of Jeremiah 3. 22. 23.) I see my self guilty of daly backslidings from god cooling affections to him, and whoarish outgoings of heart after other things. I fear my pupils formerly, and now my eas and slouth and pleasure are getting oft between christ and me; prophaness of heart and spiritual slumber which is a not savouring of the things of god, and a secret remissness in my spirituall watch, these frequently surprize me, though god be frequently jogging me by his ordinances and providences and will not suffer me to take any long and quiet sleep, but scarrs me with the terrible apparitions of my owne vileness: blessed be his name that watcheth to keep me from falling fast asleep   from all these my slumbrings and backslidings he now calls me to return, and promiseth to pardon me, and never to upbraid me of my other lovers. why my Lord Jesus is this thy voyce, whom I haue offended, neglected, slighted? thou art more righteous and faithful than I. I come at thy call. turn thou me and I shall be turned. draw me I will run after thee. o that it might be with me as in the months past, that thou wouldst restore to me the loue of my espousalls thine to me, and mine to thee and communion with thee. But why am I stared in the face with the dreadful apparitions of that sin that sin I say, a heart that cannot so much as earnestly desire such communion with thee and sence of thy loue as sometimes I have found? why am I sould into the hands of this mine enemy? Pride that also prevails over me. why goe I mourning, Lord, because of the oppression of the adversary? Is there no baulm in Gilead for these sores? no physician there that can cure these plagues? Or do thy compassions fail toward me? where are the sounding of thy bowels father? Why art thou angry with thy poor prisoner so long and shuttest out my prayers, which I haue long made for pardon and power against these sins? hast thou said to my soul seek my face in vain then? I know there are iniquitys with me, but are there not forgivenesses and plenteous redemption with thee? neither do I know that I haue wickedly departed from my god, and wilfully, at least persisted therein at any time without abasing my soul before god? why then doest thou set my sins in the light of thy countenance, Lord, and hidest from me thy face nay leavest me in the hands of my prevailing corruptions? My soul cleav's to the dust, Lord undertake for me! And as thou biddest me return, so do thou turn me from all my abominations and I shall be turned o Lord my God.

26   about the 3d day I took a good part of the day to see into the evil of my prevailing evils pride, and sensuality not savouring the grace of god and his love. Concerning which see more in the other end of this book.[14]

27   Yet on the 4th day at lecture I found my vile heart apt to be weary beforehand of the feared length of the publick ordinances: and I feel my spirit so leavened with sensuality that I cannot but be hanckering in my thoughts after creature comforts as of meat and drink &c when I should be holy intent to gods worship in religious services especially if they put me by the other. I took time to look into the evil of this also and much I did see. Athisme and not apprehending of god there present: for if god voutsafe to come and speak to me cannot I voutsafe to afford him hearing? unbeleef. for did I beleev that god were in those ordinances for my good, that would take away tediousness ingratitude, sensuality &c. Now the good Lord look down at last and here the groaning of his poor prisoner, and come and save me from the tyranny of these enemies of his as well as myne.

On the sabbath day night we set sayl. in 2 dayes we came to Martins Vinyard.[15] and were under sayl but 2 dayes from thence to the Bay, yet detained there 6 dayes by a strong Northeast wind. I look at it as great mercy that god provided so wel For us in a safe harbor at friends houses during that long storm. If we had either all that while been at sea we

[14] See pp.102–107
[15] Martha's Vineyard.

might haue had our liues in great danger: if we had been in a harbour near no plantation it had been exceeding uncomfortable; but god prevented both in mercy. When the storm was over a good harbour was but a prison to us. therefore I besought the lord earnestly and set my self to plead with god and take hold of him by faith for sutable winds to carry us toward our desired port; and god graciously heard my prayer both then, and afterward he answer'd my petitions for the continuance and renewing of that mercy, giving us a speedy passage; which answer to prayer I account a greater mercy than the thing begged by far. Hence I had ground to plead with god for greater mercys, because he had granted that to me. If I regard not iniquity in my heart god will hear me in what I ask aco. to him: but I regard not iniquity, for els god would not once and again haue heard my crys, and shewed me a signe for good.

Therefore Lord hear my crys, my sighings, my groans   bottle thou my tears wherewith I seek at the hands of a father pardon and power over my still prevailing lusts, principally pride and sensuality, want of love to thee and fervent desires after communion with thee. And do not thou continue to smoak against the prayers of thy prisoner suffering these myne iniquities to be most fearfully prevalent, when god hath been using the sharpest meanes to cure them, and kill them, and when thou hast giuen me a heart most awakened with them and earnest with thee for deliverance from them! And so my prayers for those committed to me, those children of thine whom I pray'd for strive for, hoped for, and thought that the time of gods hearing had been nigh, because he so strangely stir'd up my heart restlesly to seek their good. but loe! contrary to my hopes I find the most hopeful of them far wors than when I left them. for this my spirit was at my return sorely perplexed, that I feared my sorrow for others, would keep me from sence of my owne sin. But having indeavour'd to discharge my duty by warnings and admonitions in the fear of god my pirit is somewhat at eas in that regard. I would I could be more diseased with my unworthy carriages godward. and oh that god would once at last appear for my plenteous redemption from them. for pardon and power I see a necessity of flying to him alone. And Lord deny me not this grace whatever thou deny me. satisfy me with thy grace that my soul may learn to prize it. And for my other petition for others: why Lord 'tis thyne owne name, thyne owne interest that is ingaged. by whom shall Jacob arise? if this society ly in wickedness one generation corrupting another.

[About a page left blank]

out of 1 John 15. God did very particularly discover to me the vileness of myne owne personal distempers: in the forenoon speaking of preferring christ aboue all things. I find that although the bottom support of my heart be in god yet I cannot prize actuall communion with him at present. I cannot savour that above communion with men, therefore I am not worthy of him. In the afternoon we heard of Johns humility in seeking onely christs exaltation not his owne. I find pride so beset so trample upon my spirit in all I do (even this day I feel it) that with confusion of face I confess my self to be above measure vile. yet I haue no power either to love and prize communion with christ or to seek him and not my self in what I do. ah Lord! I am oppressed, overpowred, thy grace in me is even strangled   Lord undertake for me. I haue no strength nor might to combat with these Anakims. Lord I ly at thy feet unworthy to be helped by thee, worthy rather to be trampled on in thy fury (forasmuch as I haue trampled on and dispized christ in his glory) but remember thine owne name, thinck off thy Covenant, there is all my hope. Lord I ly downe in my shame worthy to be rejected. If thou wilt haue no pleasure in me nor any of my services, loe here I am!   whatever become of so vile a despizer of thy grace as I, though I never injoy thee, yet thou art blessed and glorious thy self   be thou Exalted for ever as thou deservest, though I be damned as I wel deserv for defrauding thee of thy glory. If I should be so, yet me thinks that would be some comfort and contentment that my god should be glorify'd though I were confounded. But I haue heard of thee by hearing of the ear to be a God of mercy pardon and plenteous redemption. let myne eyes see the such an one. hear thou therefore the groanings of thy poor prisoner that is captivated and oppressed by thine adversarys.

June 1   I was notwithstanding overborn with pride once and again in the forepart of the week, and ffound much of the venom thereof. At Watertown lecture God was pleased in some measure graciously to breath in my heart hearing Mr. Sherman upon that The pure in heart shall see God. he exhorted to labour after the assurance of gods favour, and 2ly to labor for somewhat of gods presence to see god in some glorious manifestation of himself in every ordinance and providence. though not alway to expect god to prosper (though that be desirable in its place) yet to see him even in crosses and frownes working things about for our good. to that end he exhorted to purity of heart. And thence he comforted such as mourn under, and strive against that great impurity which they find that account their sin no part of themselves, but as their enemy; they shall see god. I find my owne carnality, how I am sold under sin, and can not savour or desire communion with god, and this sensual frame most surprizeth me, when I should be nearest to god in hearing the word or in prayer. yet I look upon this and would loath it and my self for it, Lord make me so do more and more, and subdue it for me according to thy great mercy.

Since this I haue found God letting forth some little beam of his glory or drop of his sweetness into my soul, making me to rely upon a god really present with me as the stay of my soul, when creatures are all miserable comforters, and studys themselues (through troubles every way occurring) no better then vexation of spirit. he onely is my father, able to make me happy willing to make me happy in himself though for my good he disquiet me in the creature, to drive me out of that misery which I haue throwne my self into by over-esteeming the creature and under-valuing him who is my creator and my God.   2. 3

Ah Lord! what is so seely [silly] poor a wretch as I, that god should busy himself so about my good both in ordinances and providences. that thou shouldst cross and correct me to teach me wisdom, seing I should not learn it otherwise? joyn instruction to thy correction father. as thou layest on thy rod so put under thy staf to support me. pardon all my sins, giue me thy self and conformity to thy self, that's the great thing that I desire; help me to desire it more according to thy promiss wherein is all my hope.

On the sabbath day morning in private prayers I could not find my desires more earnestly carry'd after present deliverance from my owne sins, then after the conversion and salvation of my pupills: which troubled me to think that I should be more desireous of mans good than of gods glory which I daly wrong and injure with such aggravations as none can doe that yet know not god. for that that is it that provokes him, the iniquitys of his sons and daughters. But so am I sold under sin and hardness of heart that cannot groan under my iniquitys as my greatest burthen. ah Lord I am vile and poor, and sinful, helpless in my self, o take not thy good spirit from me, which may sanctify me by every ordinance of thine owne. myne eys are to the (my rock, my father) for this grace A heart to loath and labour under my sin and my self aboue any thing, and to prize the and thy glory aboue all things.

I still find pride and a deceitfulness of heart in going out of affections toward things here below, also vainity and little els in holy dutys, somewhat of frowardness or shortness of spirit, and though my sins be great, yet somewhat small but god is my trust, o take not thy spirit from me.

I meet this week with many disquieting vexations, and find my self utterly unable to carry and behaue my self in my place, confrontings therein   10 Friday

by some, and I doubt stomakings by those whome I hoped best off: I find
the spirits off all or most off from studys, and going agadding after vanity
and mispence of time; this spirit I find creeping up much in those who before I left them were most hopeful: this to repress costeth me much study
and sollicitous thoughts in the most loving way to doe it; but notwithstanding all my forethoughts I cannot perform it as I should when it comes
to. I am impotent and unable to bear the burthen of so many upon me, and
this distracts me when I should be taken up with my god, so I take his
name in vain. I find my unbeleiving heart discouraged in prayer, at least
it runns after other things, and those affections I had before in meditation
almost lost; I find afflictions without and sin pride especially and sensuality
within prevail. God is the great thing that I desire and 'tis his grace which
supports my heart, yet I cannot keep up my desires after him. He seems
not to hear or regard my prayers or indeavours either for my owne good or
the good of others. my vileness makes that labour fruitless, which haply
god would in another crowne with a blessing. ah I cannot serv not glorify
my god, therefore I am almost quiet [quite] weary, (weary me more o
God) of this world, longing after plenteous redemption from all iniquity.
ah! when shall it once be! when shall I live to thy prays and walk and
glory in the light of thy Countenance!

I haue now no confidence in the flesh. my owne conceits of my doing something for god more than others do, I see are all vain. I feel I cannot do any thing of my self, so far as god leav's me to myne owne weakness (though I contrived never so wel before hand) yet I fayl in the doing so that shame may sit in my face: yea I mar all I doe, I pul downe with
the one hand what I build up with the other   Less endeavours might have
more fruit and be of more avail, were there less self seeking in me. god
needs no service of mine: were I gone hence peradventure some other
would succeed mee whome god would more delight to bless. And although I know god can accept services that are full of manifold imper-
fections by faith in christ as, well as if they were without sin wholy: But
my actions are all so full of self seeking, self-exalting and admiring, so full
of seeking the creature or to haue others happy and my self comforted in
others happiness so much weariness in holy dutys, that I may with shame
and confusion question whether there be any true aiming at gods glory in
the most of my actions or not, and if none. and if there be no right end of
them how is there any goodness in them? or any thing that God can
owne? And if God accept them not, what profit haue I off any thing that
I do under the sun? Besides as that which is crooked who can make streight,
so my faith that is as weak as my works imperfect. others that can both

do and beleiv more god would bless more: but no marvel though he blast my indeavours, though he shut out my prayers and refuse to accept my services. But ah Lord! shall I whom thou hast formed for thy glory, not onely stain thy glorious name my self and undervalew thy grace, and offend thy good majesty, but shall my sins keep and withold thy grace from many more? shall I cumber the ground in the place of one that should do good and propagate thy glory, my self undermining the propagation thereoff by my sins making my pains unprofitable? better were it that I were out of this world than that both God and man should sustain such injury at my hand. for these things o Lord I ly down in my shame before thee.

And why do vain thoughts still lodge within me upon thy day, amidst   1 2 sabbath thy worship? ah my God, why is there yet such a prophane spirit let loose to trample my soul under foot, as that I cannot see the evils, be sensible of the plagues of my owne heart when I am waiting to hear thee speak in thy ordinances? when I should receiv good from thee I grow unsensible of my need of grace for my self: hence I mind with greater affection what concerneth others good than my owne. My heart is no sooner beginning to be awakened, affected, broken for my sins, (as it began yesterday) but my goodness (if any there be) is like the morning dew that is dried up. When I am comming to the pool, why then some wandring thoughts, some sloatful fit, or some disordered affection steps between me and the Lord Jesus before I come at him I haue no power to get, no skil or might to keep my longing desires after christ Jesus and his redemption from all my god-dishonouring and spirit grieving abominations; but whilest christ delays his comming I slumber and sleep: or I slake my thirst at some puddle or other and so ceas prizing of him. dayes weeks months pass over me, and yet I get not over the prevailing of the same corruptions; becaus little coming to christ, scanty or short desires of him, why receiv little from him, and hence return less unto him. as I haue been shown this day out of 1 John. 16.

ah Lord there is all fulness even grace for grace with thee, o send me not away empty from the but pardon, but pitty for I am oppressed by thy foes. I haue no power to help my self, but myne eyes my groanings are to thee, who hast deliver'd my soul out of the lowest hell and therefore wilt deliver me.

I find afternoon a heart full of vain wandring thoughts sottish and unaffected with my misery and sinfulness pride also. why Lord take not thy good spirit from me, which is my onely joy in the hous of my pilgrimage. o let not iniquity prevail over me! I see I am less than the least good thought or affection, cannot mourn under my wretchedness. o then make christ precious to me, in whom alone is, and from whom I hope, I pray, I wait to receiv all things.

On munday morning I found my heart upon my studys so that I knew not how to get it off whilest I was seeking god. Pride also that day and especially the next day at at [*sic*] a private meeting. ah under this my soul groanes that I would resist and cannot, I would overcome that lust which marrs my best performances, but cannot: nay cannot so much as open my mouth at sometimes to cry for help against it. ah when shall I be deliver'd from the body of this death   when shall it once be?   upon the like case as I remember at New Haven, god told me his grace should be sufficient for me. sufficient to accept of me and my performances for christs sake; sufficient to forgiue my backslidings

Communion with god, conformity to god are the 2 great things which my soul in some poore measure longs after this morning and I desire to mourn more after them.

19   I set some time apart of the last day to look over my life and former sins in way of preparation to the sacrament but could find little sutable affection and mourning for the many sins and greivous that I stand guilty of before god.

I was affraid of drawing neer god in so holy an ordinance for at sometimes I find no power at all to prize the Lord christ and reconciliation by him. o if god leav me to the prophaness of my heart as I deserv he should, I can valew him no more than the dry dust I tread upon. And I have found my heart so often left to the prevailing of this prophanness, for this caus am I affraid   If my heart deceiv me not, it is ready to make such objections as these

In the time of hearing the word I found the same dead sensuall frame of heart in me getting ground of me more than before I came to the meeting. Mr. Mitchel shew'd the danger and the vile sin of a careless spirit that hath little or no appetite unto christ and communion with him   such frustrate the very end of the ordinance which is communion. why Lord thou seest and I see that this is my frame. And thereby I am unfit unworthy to receiv thee, if thou leav me I shall but eat and drink to my self damnation. o Lord I am affraid of this. true I cannot love thee, and am therefore vile exceeding vile, and the more vile by how much the less affected with it, sensible of it. And this sin with my pride were enough to sink me for ever had I no more to answer for. But the more helpless and hopeless in my self father, why I haue the more need of thy christ to become all unto me: and therefore I desire to fly unto him although unfit to receiv him that he may make me fit. I see a need of whole christ and do desire him, help my want of desires   open thou my mouth wide and then fill it with thy son. I need him, and therefore Lord according to thy free and gracious offer and command I desire to take him, as a prophet to reveal the fathers glory to me, that god may be most glorious in my eys; I can see no glory in thee Lord! except thy onely begotten son reveal thee. I desire him as my onely priest and propitiation, ah I haue daly sins and therefore want him to make a daly attonement, that my sins may not separate between mee and my god, and cause him and his spirit whose visitations preserv my spirit to depart from me; thats my death, that I am affraid of. that I may be accepted for his sake, who in and of my self deserv onely condemnation. I desire him for my king that he may subdue all the enmity of heart against him, that I may no longer loath him without a caus, nor love other things above him. that he may subdue my unconquerable corruptions pride, and whoarish affections; which I find so prevalent, as that I despair in and off my self to subdue them. I might say with David I shall surely one day fall by the hand of Saul of my whoarish affections, which eat out all actuall love to god or relish of his wayes, or very nigh: did not god reviue me a little by his grace at some seasons, by an almighty power   no less can doe it. And did not he this day and formerly ingage (and seal to his ingagement) that if I would receiv his son whom he offered freely to me why he would enter into an Everlasting Covenant that should not be broken by himself: neither would he suffer it to be utterly broken by me. ah riches of godlike grace! let it be to thy poor creture according to thy good word. let christ be mine let me be his alone. I come to thee to make me every day more willing it should be so. and now o that I had a heart to live upon thee to liue to thee that I could go away and sin no more. But woe and alas what vain thoughts? what weariness of gods service prevails in me, which I haue no power to overcome? what pride. innumerable evils compass me about, and they are too hard for me. but god be thank't through Jesus christ who giues so vile a sinner hopes of reconciliation and favour with himself notwithstanding my owne iniquity's. Amen Lord so let it be!

O Lord what hankering after creature comforts when I am in thy presence seeking of thee   Thoughts running after them and I cant get them off   What an uncontrollable power of pride again and again overbearing me misspence of time I fear that is not attending my work in the season I fear lest greiving of thy spirit and quenching its motions   O take it not from me hide not thy face set not my secret sins in the light of thy countenance   I find vanity everywhere beside

Let me find rest and peace in thee   Speak peace to me that I may return no more to folly   O what need have I of a savior to make atonement for such great abominations   O let me have him   Accept me in him   And the more neglect of business I have upon me which endanger the drawing of my heart from the fear and love of God   I beseech thee I beseech thee let the power of my Lord be the more great in keeping alive the love of God in my soul and desire after communion with thee   This request I put up from the bottom of my soul for I am afraid of my own deceitful heart.

22   I find a heart so dead, and hard in Every ordinance even at the lecture this 4th day and thoughts so wandring in private dutys, and such an unsavoury spirit that cannot prize love desire communion with christ and mourn for my provoking him: and so much pride I haue found prevailing this week, such a spirit of whoardoms and departure from god that I haue no power against: so that I find an infinite need of the Lord Jesus to reconcile me every day to the father. and I am affraid of my owne vile heart that I shall one day fall by the hand of Saul; and these feares would haue wrought in me much discouragement peradventure, if the Lord had not so lately confirmed his gift of christ to me, and renewed my closing with him, for this very end to deliver me from this iniquity. ah Lord! when shall it once be my trust and my onely hope and help   fail me not in a time of need. it hath been and is my fervent desire that the Lord would keep my spirit from being stoln from him by my manifould occasions and business as I shall certainly daly be without his grace, by his grace onely I stand.

24 Friday   *John Haines one of my pupils having formerly desired liberty to go toward Ipswich and being denied by me (for I was afraid of him and of that degeneracy which I to my grief saw in him since my return) I say he went away on the 2d day to Salem without my leave or either the President's knowledge or mine and stayed out till the 5th day night and then came not to give any account of his journey nor to obey their commendation to me that sent them to him. The thing was very exercising and grievous to me from the fact that one that had been of such hopes did now quite fail my expectation in such wise. Upon his return this 6th day I took occasion to speak to him though having premeditated a convicting discourse and having set myself to find out arguments to wrestle with the Lord for him and others and having besought the Lord seriously beforehand and desired him not for my sins to withold his blessing from others and from this whole society. I told him not only of his evil carriages in this business (which indeed be too apparent) and of his breach of his own engagement at his admission and his endeavoring to disable me from rending an account of him either to god or man as I accounted myself solemnly charged to do but also of the great grief he put both me and others of his friends*

to in seeing our expectations and hopes so strangely failed and he so suddenly altered from what he sometimes seemed at least to be. I told him that danger of backsliding from former attainments how Satan enters in with no spirits worse than himself and the latter end of that may become worse than his beginning. I told him of the dog returning to his vomit and the sow to her wallowing &c. Not myself only but others had had great hopes of his towardliness and thereby been much endeared to him and could not but be so still but now both myself and others (who had spoken to me so much concerning him) feared or rather saw it was not with him as formerly. I told him how sad it would be to his parents to hear another report of him than I had given them before. But I concluded if he thought such things as these were for his own honor that they would be for his future comfort that they would be well pleasing to God who goes on and prospers. &c. He wept and seemed much affected at my speech. I wished him not [to] be discouraged at it but consider seriously of those things which I spoke out of the greatness of my love and sorrow that it should be otherwise with him than formerly. He thanked me for my love and said he hoped God would do him good by what I had said to him in his time   I prayed that God might do so. I asked him further if himself did not see that to be true that I had spoken to him that his heart was gone after pleasure and off from those good ways he had sometimes walked in and he answered somewhat in way of assent thereto fearing that it was. I told him also of the dangers of pleasure and how they had like to have been my ruin   Knowing the danger of them therefore I dissuade both myself and others. And so I bade him farewell. But that very evening he was again at play I think among the students and when he saw me coming he slinked home and left his game whereby I gather that he is more afraid of me a poor sinful worm than of God and I am sorry that so solemn a warning and so efficacious for the present should have lost its power so soon. ah Lord why dost thou shut out my prayers both for my self and others? I haue transgressed and rebelled and thou hast not pardoned. I know I am not worthy to haue power over my owne lusts, nor to see thy grace powred upon any of mine. yet Lord cannot the Lord Jesus make my sinful prayers and tears and endeavours as acceptable as anothers? or if that will not be graunted, (as lord why may it not seing I plead onely free grace which thy self gives me an intrest in) yet arise for thine owne sake, and cause thy face to shine upon us, turn us again our god and we shall be saved. all my springs and hope is in thee, o deny me not thy self!

I set my self again this day to wrestle with the Lord for my self and then   25
for my pupils and the Lord did pretty much inlarge my heart in crying to
him. But still I see the Lord shutting out my prayers and refusing to hear
for he whom in special I pray'd for, I heard in the forenoon with ill company playing musick, though I had so solemnly warn'd him but yesterday of

letting his spirit go after pleasures. And again I see light and vain carriage in him just at night on this last day at even.[16] For these things my heart is fill'd and almost sunk with sorrow and my bowels are turned within me; ah Lord how long, how long wilt thou shut out my prayers?

(sabbath
26/

My sins are especially Pride, weariness of gods ordinances, whorish heart (which having lost the feeling of my owne evils looseth its sence of a daly need of christ for my self) unbeleif. for my heart and eyes are even ready to fail with waiting for the Lords Salvation seing I find god denying me both power over my owne distempers, and they are ready to get ground on me whilest I am praying for gods glory and others good: and also he refuseth to comfort me with the returns of his spirit to our society which alas is almost quite gone I fear, and it may be sayd of almost all of us god is not here. we who are set apart for god's glory, why god and godliness are clean vanish't from among us. None stirs up himself to take hould of a god departing, but every one endeavouring to drive him away yea even off those few that profess the Lord, I wish there were not falling off from him and his worship at least cooling in affections to him, I excuse not myself. Those that were hopeful heretofore, and whom my soul longed to have seen made exemplary in their places to succeders are now become sensual as others if not corrupters of others. These evils are upon us and none know's how long? I cry to the Lord in this respect but he is so far from hearing, that he seems angry with my prayers, and whilest I seek him for others I loose him and my love to him my self, and by my whoardoms hinder that glory of god and good of others that I longed for. shall not my eyes run down with tears, and my heart and bowels be oppressed with sorrow for these things till the Lord look down from heaven and have mercy? but ah Lord! when shall that be? for thou hast cast us off and forsaken us, and who knowes where thy displeasure will end? just art thou o Lord in all that has come upon us; yet remember mercy and think of thyne owne name.

June 26

In the forenoon on the Lords day Mr. Collins[17] preaching 1 John. 3. 3. he that hath this hope purifys himself &c. I found my heart very dead and little stird at the mention and particularizing the glory to come; much of the ould frame; least sight of gods glory or of glory in it when 'tis nearest. yet at home in after meditations at noon and the next day it pleased god

---

[16] The Puritan sabbath began at sundown on Saturday night, hence "light and vain carriage" at this time was a breach of the sabbath.

[17] John Collins graduated from Harvard in 1649, joined the church at Cambridge (see his "relation" below, p. ??), taught at Harvard and preached for a time. In 1653 he went to England where he became famous as pastor of a church in London.

shew me some little glimpse of his glory, and to let me feel a drop of the sweetness of his love and communion with him. yet after this a munday my spirit was almost quite discouraged and soul and body both ready to quail, because of my sorrows for what mine eyes daly behould in others sins and mispence of their precious hours. this evening I haue found a little reviving and cheering up of my spirit in god. o how precious art thou o never failing, ever loving, freely-pardoning, Compassionately-pittying father, when others do not pitty, cannot help; o be thou my portion, for I have none els, help me to joy in thee alone o god of my Salvation, make, make I beseech thee christ precious and sin bitter (my own sin) unto me!

Tuesday was a private fast. I was very dead hearted in the beginning of the day, the night before. In publick it pleased the Lord to powre upon me some measure of affection. but now woe is me! how incurable is my wound that wilest I am confessing and shaming my self before god for my pride and sensuality, and security, even then pride of gods gifts (good affections) ariseth. No marvel then if god visite with bodily weakness to keep it downe, no marvail, though he blast my endeavours and make the colledge and country about me fare the worse for my sake. though he punish my barrenness with publick drought: though he say of this poor society: I haue shown such and such favour to one of you, and loe! he loath's me, cares not for me, robs me of my glory, and all this for my love; Ile shew you no more mercy, my spirit shall strive with no more of you. Thus I can pul down wrath and destroy my self and all about me, but to do good I haue no knowledge. Lord I am vile, but thou art gracious, turn to me rather in mercy than in displeasure. ah let not my sins fall upon others of thy people. fail not their hopes, stain not thy owne glory for my sake.

script. 30th

I am still affraid that my sorrow for sin should not be true because I find such vehement and unappeaseable affections toward others longing, striving, praying for their good; and yet so little mourning and fighting against and restless striving for deliverance from my owne prevailing iniquitys. pride and vain thoughts weariness of gods service &c. The like feares were renew'd and increased in the publick ordinances Mr. Dunster preaching how any lust of other things though lawful and a duty in themselves any inordinate immoderate desire chokes the word. I found again such an utter impotency of spirit to desire more communion with and conformity to christ, and to mourn under the want thereof as my greatest evil. thou Lord requirest that I have and loath and mourn under sin as my daly greatest evil. I desire to do but cannot: Nay I cannot keep up those desires. ah! Lord saue me or I perish. my life is hid with thee, thither I come for it o send me not empty away! God let me se in the forenoon that two violent im-

Sabbath July 3

petuous desiring of lawful things and unseasonable desireing them becomes a lust when the soul is even ready to dy away if it haue them not presently. both these I am guilty of in reference to my pupils good. The latter of them to my shame this day. For Afternoon the Lord spake very sutably to my condition, namely to set before me the greatness of the sins of the godly being committed against father Son and holy ghost actually communicating themselves in greatest love, dwelling in and with the soul &c. Here though I did approve of the truth and se it sutable to me, yet I could not get my heart out of that frame to desire that the Lord would rather speak some sutable word to my pupils. O confounding vileness of an unthankful, impenitent heart! what was this but to say to the Lord (when he sent his spirit, for ought I know in so sutable a word to have wrought all that grace in me that I have long bin groaning after) depart from me and speak to some other that have more need of thee for the present then I? Is this with humble thanks to adore that grace of god that fits a word to my souls necessity? is this with fear and trembling to work out myne owne Salvation when god is affording speciall means and speaking to me? Is this to pant after the Lord and conformity to him, as being deeply apprehensive of the death, the poison and I feel frequently (and this day feel) working in my soul? Have others need of gods present grace that sin onely against gods common love, and haue I that sin against special love (and am heard hearted and unaffected with my sin) haue I no need of present pardon, and of present plenteous redemption? Truely I deserv that god should visit me in his ordinances noe more, but go to those that prize and need him more. How justly might the Lord leav me in the hand of myne iniquitys (which my soul abhors) pride and despizing of communion with christ, seing I put from me salvation when it came so near me? Lord Jesus I ly down in my shame before the deserving to be destroy'd. Nothing in me but what draw's on ruine with cart ropes. but when I ey thy sure covenant, as I am asham'd of my owne faithlesness, so thy truth giues me hope that thou wilt not leav my soul in the grave, nor suffer thy redeemed to see corruption. therefore I lift up my heart with my hands to a father in christ Jesus begging for pardon and redemption from all those iniquitys and for continuance of this desire   my self can do, desire, will no good thing. ah Lord do not thou fail me who art my trust and blessed be thy great name which thou hast given such a vile wretch to trust in. o that I might no more dishonour it!

4.5.   *In the 2 next days I found so much of a spirit of pride and secret joying in some conceived excellence in my self which is too hard for me and I cant prevail over and also so much secret vice and vain thoughts in holy duties and thereby weariness of them and such filthy lust also flowing from my fond affection to my pupils whiles in their presence on the third day after noon that I confess myself an object of God's loathing as my sin is of my own and pray God make it so more to me*

I have much business lies upon me, that requires much of my thoughts and strength; and I have not so much free time for musing off the things of god as perhaps I should. and my heart is so long composing to any serious thoughts and so soon out of a good frame again. I am so soon lost in my affections. I find such a bent of spirit to feed my self with fore-contrivances for my owne self and work or for my pupils good, and so unable to do in that kind what god requires without losing my love to my god and communion with him. that my soul is affraid within me of my owne spirit of whoardoms. I can meddle with nothing but I mar it, and lose my self, and griev the spirit of my god: and find a dead heart that cannot griev for it when I have done. I am affraid to follow close my ordinary studys, because my heart is so stouln away with them, and I cannot prize the presence of god more than them, I mean his outward services. much unbelief therefore that cannot expect to meet him whom my soul desires in wayes of his owne. *I should say I shall one day surely fall to the hand of Saul were I left to myself. But when my foot is almost gone why thy right hand O Lord upholds me and thy visitation preserves my spirit   O therefore take not take not I beseech thee thy holy spirit from me though I grieve it   O give a new heart a circumcized heart to love the harking to thy convenant though I deserve no grace from thee   Give me not to my own heart's lusts for I am thy possession purchased by thee   I have given up myself unto thee   O do not cast me off   My heart is evil and sinful yea but thy truth is firm and everlasting and that is the ground of all my hope and all my salvation   My other hopes are but like a spider web. Why blessed be thy name that gives me leave and any desire to hope in thy self   Increase these desires I pray thee and fail not my hopes   Preserve me in thy tender mercy that neglect of business and cares nor lust of other things check my affection to thee that is my great fear   make it my daily care.*

I am the last night and this morning still excedingly affraid of a lukewarm prophane indifferency of affection toward god and his grace which seizeth upon me sometimes when I should be nearest to him. therefore I cry to the Lord according to his promise that he would not suffer his children to be murderd before his eys as I am in fear of: I feel death creeping into and seizing upon my soul ever and anon. I beg and groan to the Lord to redeem me from all iniquity and from all confidence in my self or the creature, and god promises 14 Hosea to heal the backslidings of such. I will therefore wait and hope and strive for this salvation

I take it as a fruit of gods tender love that he is now and then awakening me with the vileness of my owne heart to look about me to the things of my owne peace that he makes me to see that I haue need of a redeeming kinsman of a daly peace maker: though it be matter of shame and confusion when I feel such an Ocean of deadly poyson in my heart as sometimes discovers it self in pride, sometimes in secret letting out of my affections to my studys more than god and communion with him, not savouring the things of god, and therefore weariness of his service   Horrible ingratitude when god offers me his presence and communion, that I had rather be in the bosom of any thing any vanity than of him thus grieving his spirit to be so slighted by one whom of all others he might expect most fear and love. unbeleef. impeniency that cannot mourn bitterly for those things, great sins but small sorrow. And I deserv that god should hearden my heart because I put from me his grace the last sabbath when he came in so sutable a word to soften it. these are my plagues that none can heal. but blessed be god that has layd up all fulness in christ for poor needy indigent sinners; and bids me come to him empty (ay so Lord I must come   I cannot of my self prize or desire thy grace or maintain my desire thou knowest, o pitty me) come freely, o riches of grace! I can merit nothing but wrath   draw me, I will run after the; all my hope is in thee. help me with patience and continued constant desires to wait on thee.

The Lord in some measure helped me to attend on him this day free from those doting affections to others that I use to have and did somewhat speak suitable truths to my need and brought them home to me in some measure   I blessed him for anything   I beseech him pardon that infinite defect of a right frame and worldly repentance and faith which there should have been   I desire to come to him without anything for all things. In the afternoon the Lord brought home to my conscience the sin of lying at one special time [at] Hartford and make me somewhat troubled in spirit to think what God required of me whether to confess it to man or no and whether it might not be of evil consequence and on this occasion I looked over my former abominations and have cause to wonder that I do enjoy any quiet day in this world that I am not made a barrier to myself to provision of this horrid iniquity that I have sold myself to   The Lord be blessed and Lord pity me   And give a heart to live closely with thee and do not set my old iniquity in the light of thy countenance. Supply my wants temporal and spiritual and heal my soul and body for both are very loath and unable to do thy service.

I was this week at 2 lectures the one treating of the glorious priviledge of the sons of god, and how foolish we are in not making the thoughts of those truths the food of our soul, god in measure breathed into my soul therein; also at Boston lecture. where was held forth the readiness of all grace in christ to all the souls want. But pride sundry times monstrously prevailed; I was (and still desire to continue so) ashamed and confounded before the Lord for this abomination. My proneness to satisfy my soul in my study's or pupills progress, or any thing without god is the daly fear of my soul; the secret pitfall that (as I am most unawares caught with so) fills me with fear so that I dare not go on sometimes in my studys as my over eager spirit would carry me, without recalling myself to muse of the things of god. But alas! I find little of god breathing in my prayers or meditations, little love to the lord Jesus (though I daly seek it as my great request) much vain thoughts, weariness, and unbeleif. 'tis not with me as in times past, when I could find sweet repose for a weary soul in christs bosom. And 'tis just with the Lord it should be so, I have despiz'd communion with him, (which frame my heart is affraid to think of, much more to feel) communion is in a great measure witheld from me, yea and a heart to prize and long after it many times is deny'd me, I seek and beg it, yet cannot find it. I know I deserv to have christ and all his grace hid from me. But merciful father in christ my Lord! didst not thou the god of truth ingage to put into me the spirit of a son (in the day of thy Covenant with me) and loe the spirit of a Devil, the very poison of Hel it self in that heart which should be the temple of the holy-ghost. Canst thou indure to see thine owne inheritance layd wast? thine owne temple poluted? thine owne children murdered? can the god of mercy and faithfulness stand by and see a poor wretch overborn by his too strong adversarys, stretching out his feeble hands to thee not onely his maker, but his sworn redeemer, and wilt thou suffer him to perish without help? it cannot be. why awake o arm of the Lord, put on strength (o god my strength) come speedily to my succour, make no tarrying. for thyne owne Covenant and glory (which are my hope when readie to quail) send me thy saving health!

My soul waits for some of those sweet meetings that sometimes I haue   Sabbath 17
had with the Lord Jesus. In the forenoon god awakned me with feares and disquietments in reference to an untrueth that formerly long agoe I had told, vizt, that *I knew nothing of Mister Mildmay's*[18] *sword nor who had it when I think Sir Cotton*[19] *had it and I knew it* I questioned whether the Lord

[18] Possibly William Mildmay, son of Sir Henry Mildmay of Graces in Essex, who was sent over from England to be educated at Harvard and who graduated with the class of 1647.

[19] Probably Seaborn Cotton, oldest son of the Reverend John Cotton of Boston, who was born at sea on the way to New England in 1633. He graduated from Harvard in 1651, in the same class with Wigglesworth, and became minister of the church at Hampton, New Hampshire. The use of the title "Sir" with the surname indicates that at the time of which Wigglesworth was speaking Cotton had received his bachelor's degree but was continuing at the college in order to become a Master of Arts.

call'd me now to speak of so triviall a thing as this is when as I partly *think it was found out again and carried away with [him] hence and whether I be called to rack in a business so old. My spirit was somewhat quieted in reference to that* God gave me also some incouragement from the markes giv'n of good ground, sundry of them I hope I can owne in some measure before god.

Afternoon again god suffred much disquietment to distract my spirit and hinder my edification in reference to an omission of somewhat which I knew not whither a duty or no. I cry'd to the Lord in the anguish of my soul at the meeting, and he remov'd the temptation immediatly after my coming home. o blessed be his name! Lord teach me thy way, I will walk in all thy good paths, onely unite my heart to fear thy name. And let the joy of the Lord be my strength. return therefore in tender mercys to my soul, lift up the light of thy countenance though I deserv it not, yet do it for thy own name and glory: why should I live in thy world and haue no heart to glorify thee? change therefore I beseech the my heart, and put the living, active, constant love and fear of god into my soul, and through those preserv me to thy heavenly Kingdom from all apostacy in actions or affection, to which I am so dangerously inclined!   thou art my trust.

18   On the 2d day I found pride together with sleighthing one with whome I disputed, and two much peremptoriness in speech: and this although god had that very morning let my doutful conscience perplex me to shew me my folly, and what need I had to get and keep near god.

19   Tuesday I felt pride again prevail several times, though in some measure I hope withstood, but it's two hard for me. And eager impetuos pursuit of my studys, to get my manifould businesses rid out of hand. this I am exceedingly affraid off, I cry to god against, and dare not without so doing goe on constantly in my studys, for fear of losing my self and my heart. And yet how do I lose it notwithstanding? How little love to the Lord Jesus maintained? ah Lord pardon, and be speedy for my releif.

20   I am affraid of losing Christ and being separated from him by sin, but I cannot mourn for it kindly as it wrongs and greives god. Notwithstanding the Lord was graciously present this day in his ordinances awakening in the former part for my sensuality relishing more sweetness in the creature than christ, for by my weariness sometimes in or backwardness to seeking of him to purpose, thereby dispizing christ and all his grace, o monstrous iniquity, partly also incouraging from the testimonies of my conscience to me in somethings. partly perswading my heart (I hope truely to renew my closing with christ: whole christ god wil'd me to receiv with all my heart, parting with lusts absolutely for him, with the word and all lawfull things

comparatively making him onely, continually my trust my rest my joy for ever. Lord such a christ is he whom my soul so desires to close with. this christ and such affections to him I want I desire, help my want of desire and forgive it. owne me in him. him let me have or els I dy I have undone my self by my iniquitys, by my daly (and this day's) pride and spirituall whoardoms. let it be possible with the for christs sake to heal all my backslidings and supply all my inward (especially) and also outward pinching wants I will wait for thy salvation. onely let me neither faint through impatiency and unbeleif, nor ceas seeking through sensuality, which I greatly fear!

Still I find pride monstrously daly prevailing especially in dispute, impatiency of spirit not to carry all before me &c. a heart fearfully prone to lose my love to god, to be weary of his ordinances to think the time much that I spend in his presence, and indeed a little time will do nothing at my heard heart. 23

I was on friday betwixt desires to issue more of my business and fear least I should then neglect god and attendance of him, much exercised. at last I threw all aside and god gaue me a few sweet thoughts of him self. But o Ephraim thy goodness is as the morning dew! my body is almost overcome with the violent heat, Lord fit me for thy service and day; make it precious pleasant, not tedious to me. speak thou to my heart that I may not fail nor fall off any more to folly; that I may be sensible how much better thy presence is than the bosom of other lovers.

God hath all this day marvelously suted his word to my condition. telling me of all fulness in christ inviting and directing to him; stirring up to prize him &c. as if the Lord had spent the most of this day purposely for me, and spoke onely to me. yet ah! little sutable affection to such great wants, to so gracious words. Heart dead, senseless of my own wants and woes when god was revealing his grace. I cannot yet get over that plague of seing and feeling no present necessity of grace from christ. I had sore conflict with feares, that I could more easily bear the denyall of present delivery from my sins and prevailing evils, than from this temporall judgement of drought. As also that I desired when god was speaking to me, that somewhat might be sayd that might concern and do good to my pupills, which I am exceedingly affraid had somewhat of the prophane spirit concerning which vid. June 3.

Afternoon I had some thought there might be appointed a Fast in reference to the drought, that I had a great conflict with my owne spirit to get my spirit so off from my ordinary studys as to be in any sort willing solemnly to spend time to seek the Lord. These are the plagues that my soul lies under, and a hard heart and much unbelief added unto all, and weariness apt to seize me, (though I thank god I hope it prevailes less this day than many times) in seeking god which is the onely meanes to obtain redress

30
6th *day*   My spirit is now seized upon with feares and misgivings: I find such cause of jealousy over my owne self in regard of my proness to and often sinning against the lord by inordinate desire after dispatching and gaining much in my ordinary study's. When I would set myself to meditate on god and christ and salvation by him I am (do what I can) soon wearied with intending of thoughts that way; On the other side I dare not giue them liberty to run long after contrivances and hopes in the creature; yet they outrun me every day here. this makes me affraid; this makes that I cannot se my studys and paines performed for and accepted by god, because so much love to my studys and so little to god himself. Yet blessed be his name that lets me not be at rest in the bosom off the creature, but exerciseth me with often feares of losing himself. When he hides away his face I am troubled how ever other things fare Why father deliver me from the evil man my self, I betake my self to thy strength for sesonable help; be not to me as waters that fayl. I was twice at Boston this week. both times provoking the Lord by pride. yet the former day god heard my earnest prayer for supply of mony that I might discharge my debts according to his command. yet to abase me (as it did) he suffred me to lose a bill that was made for 32 li that might have prov'd some loss perhaps. Yet I pray'd to him again; he heard me, and restored it the next day but one. why Lord hear my prayer for grace to liue upon the, and to thee and to delight in the; is not that as acceptable a petition as either of those? is it not as much for thy glory, for my necessary good? give then I beseech the such grace for the future, pardon the iniquity thats past, pitty me that am helpless in my self, neither can keep aliue my desires after thy help.

Yesterday afternoon (meeting with some very disrespectful carriage from a student) my soul I hope did in some poor measure long for and relish sweetness in the Lord himself. And I hope there are true groanings after him in some small measure this morning I desire to mourn and lament that I can desire him so little and I am afraid of my vile heart that is apt to lose all affection to him when I should be nearest to him waiting for his salvation because my goodness is but as the morning dew O Lord hear my poor chatterings in this respect and for thy name sake deliver me

31   God is still teaching me how to come to him to doe all for me and to speed. as if he preach't to none but me from Sabbath to Sabbath. what a stupid heart have I that gets so little ground of my corruptions by all these meanes? I hope the Lord helpt me some little more than usually against that stupid frame of my heart that cannot prize christ. yet I found such deadness so little mourning for my great iniquitys (as committed against a gracious god), as made me fear my state, and not know how to evidence it to my self. Yet I conclude at length; where there has bin such a degree of humiliation as to make me goe out of my self sin and world for all grace. in the unfained desires of my soul, there is true conversion. But this there has bin often. ergo[20] that is true repentance that drives the soul to christ onely for that and all other grace; I have been daly fain to fly to christ alone for all good; ergo god accepts this (notwithstanding my daly whoar-doms) as renewed repentance. 'Tis true I cannot find power to get rid of my great iniquity why but christ hath it for all comers to him. yea but my very sence of my need of him is daly decaying; ergo he will cast me off as a despizer. no but though I cannot prize christ nor redemption by him, nor maintain a good desire to him, yet he that uphold's all things by the word of his power hath undertaken to uphold me and his grace in me; blessed therefore be god for Jesus christ. he will give Repentance to Israel and remission of sins.

I cannot prevail against that cursed frame to think the time long that I spend in reading gods word. Pride and sensuall affections outgoings of heart after my studys again get head. My heart even blesseth god when he lets me meet with crosses in the creture for then is the creatour most sweet and desirable. my soul and my spirit within me desires him, and is affraid of losing him, by my daly losing my desires to him. why I should not see such a daly necessity of a saviour if I had power to prize a saviour in my hands. Reserv thou blessed father the power in thy owne hands, but yet send not me away empty, when I seek for supplys of strength to liue with, upon, and unto god

August 1

Tuesday. I find my old plague sores still running therefore I am affraid because my very love to the Lord Jesus I haue no power to retain; I cannot but hanker after my studys whilest I am reading gods word: pride also gets ground of me. Lord Jesus if thou canst do any thing (and I know thou canst do all things) help me. The Lord made me pretty earnest with him this morning for redemption from these lusts, and I will wait for his answer, I am not worthy of any.

2

In the later part of the week the same spirit of pride and cooling of love to the Lord Jesus, immoderate outgoings of my heart to other things: and though shame for them to drive me from god, yet little true godly sorrow to drive me to god. yet I do daly endeavour in some weak measure to

6t

[20] This word is abbreviated throughout the manuscript thus: gô.

make my peace with god, and to lay up all my hope in his mercy. I remember the sweet tasts I have had of him (a dramm whereof that was very sweet I had the last Last day) and my soul would long after the like, but I am not able. ah Lord when wil thy salvation appear? how long shall I be as those that are dead long agoe? how long shall I cry and thou wilt not hear? shall I be altogether like those that thou hast giv'n over to their lusts? Lord thou owest me nothing. yea but I owe thee much. when shall I be inabled to pay it thee? oh that I could answer thyne expectations of me! remember thy covenant with me, and do it for thy name sake, though there be none els to help me.

7   Exceeding gracious was my god on the sabbath in speaking punctually to my particular needs again, and such was the scope of the whole dayes exercise to teach me to prize christ, and to incourage to seek to him for supplys and to walk humbly with him   some good measure of affection the Lord wrought in my heart in the forenoon especially, but multitudes of vain thoughts crouded in upon me in the forepart of the sabbath.

munday we disputed and I had singular assistance from god, but ah! sinful soul I cannot giue god the glory, but make his grace to serv my owne pride and vainglory and whorish departures from him. this I fear'd before hand and pray'd against, but according to my feares it came upon me. yet in the Evening the Lord took of my affections in some measure from the creatures and made me long after grace and favour with my god, and to rest my weary sinful soul in the bosom of a saviour.

I found very much pride the rest of the week prevailing sundry times and a spirit that lost my love to religious dutys that grew to weary of them, and I could do no other: this I spread before god as my fears especially this latter and and [*sic*] my plagues

Sabbath
14 *day*   Vain thoughts exceedingly prevail'd in the beginning of the day especially fears of being lead into temptation by company that we had to dinner more than ordinary, but the Lord helpt me to divert the discourse. In the afternoon god helpt me with more affection: christ was held out; off all others I need him most, my heart answers, thee Lord Jesus my soul needs and would fain with open mouth intertain; but my desires are not in my own hand, oh kindle in me glorious esteem of this glorious saviour, whom I hear the father giues welcome intertainment to in heav'n, let not me sleight him upon earth. The desires of my soul are to thy name and the remembrance of thee: that I may have thy favour which is better than life, thy assistance also in my studys (I feel my owne insufficiency   every thing becomes a snare to mee) but especially grace I beg to walk with god in the world among a perverse generation; for Jesus christ his merit and

intercession, for thine owne everlasting love, and promiss and thy glory which I would seek   deny it me not o my father and my god!

The 2d and 3d day as I found less outbreakings of sin, so I felt little heart breaking for sin: much assistance in my studys and I hope my heart in some measure caryed to seek my rest beyond them. Especially on the 3d day at night hearing some things which I had spoken to my pupils with derision reiterated among the scolars I betook my self to the Lord to be my portion.

4th day I heard at Cambridge lecture the greatness of sin being committed against the striving of gods spirit; I had much adoe to get my spirit off from minding what concern'd others to apply things to my self; though I endeavour'd it yet I found little melting affection. I took all the time between the end of the sermon and prayers at college to muse and pray: desiring that I might mourn for my ould fearful quenchings of gods spirit and these more aggravated despizings of christ of later times, though I could se nobody els affected with the word. I saw matter of amazement in looking into former and present vileness: yet Lord pardon my hard-heartedness and take not thy good spirit from me.   forgive also this evenings pride, and let it be possible with thee to subdue my iniquitys.

On friday I consulted most of the day about college affairs being much exercised with contumacious and disrespective negligent carriages of my pupils. In contrivances for redress I fear my heart rested too much: pride in discours together with sleighting and not honouring superiours prevaile extreemly; and also vain distractions in prayer.

ultimus dies/   I am much perplexed about my pupils and how to carry to them, but I cannot attain a broken heart for the same carriages in my self to my god: I would make god my resting place, but my want of repentance hinder's me.

On the sabbath my desire was that my soul might rest in the bosom of god; though I could attain little of it. God spake very sutably to me and tould me of many occasions whereupon men refuse christ, but I hope my heart approves off a christ upon those terms which the gospel offers, and that desires my heart may be made like gods rule, not that changed according to my hearts desire. He tould me the way to come to christ both for justifying and sanctifying grace; in that son of his grace I find comfort and incouragement to hope in him for pardon and power though I find in my self that which maketh me affraid and ashamed namely a spirit of whoardoms.

Some incouragement and strengthning of faith I found when I had been in his presence from his free justifying grace to all beleeving sinners.

24   Pride much prevalent: and dying away of affections toward the Lord
Jesus, and vain distractions in prayer   Lord when shall it be otherwise?
when shall it once be?   blessed be god for Jesus christ my hope.   blessed be
god for keeping aliue a spirit of great fear least I should lose my heart in the
pursuit of other things   oh grant that I may not!

25   Wednesday. distractions in holy dutys were the prevaling evil in me.
I desire to aggravate against my self my sin, and fly onely to the blood of
Jesus. And the more dead and hard hearted I am, the more rich is that
grace of thine father that will accept me in thy son, notwithstanding: god
mightily assisted me in my studys this day.

Because I find such deadness off affection to the Lord Jesus and such
weariness off, at least want of delight in his service, together with so little
hatred of and humiliation for these sins; these things sit pretty close upon
my spirit this morning and make me affraid of my owne state. for I not
onely am daly captivated by my iniquitys, but I am prone (which I most
exceedingly and daly fear least I should be separated from christ thereby,
as I deserv) to feel no necessity of the Lord Jesus to redeem me therefrom.
I therefore am the more earnest for redemption from my spirit of whoardoms, because I feel I haue not power to keep desires after such a mercy.
Lord art not thou as ready to giue me off thy spirit, as I am to giue If I
could my spirit to all my pupils? why lord redeem and save me   thou art
my tutour, my father shut not out my prayers, deliver me above all things
from that evil man my self and my spirit of backsliding.

27   Friday and Saturday. I find my spirit very apt to be gone off from delight in god, to please my self with my owne devices and contrivances. *I
found myself taken in some falsity of speech on the Lord's Day by way of com-
pliment though I am not able to justify it   I condemn myself for it before God
and desire to aggravate my sin against myself   Lord lay it not to my charge.* I am
much perplexed in spirit because I am both in a strait how to answer Mr.
Stones motion;[21] and attend my fathers counsel. I know not what gods
mind may be, I am in the dark. Also I meet with fears of wants and fayling
of necessary winter supplys for cloathing: I desire and endeavour to
strengthen my faith in god. but my sins darken my evidences of his love,
Lord forgive and heal them, and supply these.

28   Sabbath day morning in prayers god helpt me to wrestle with him with
some earnestness for sanctifying grace that I may glorify him; and for as-

---

[21] It is not clear from the diary what the elder Wigglesworth's counsel may have been,
but "Mr. Stones motion" was evidently the offer of a position as assistant or possibly
as a colleague in the church at Hartford, where Samuel Stone was minister. This offer
is again referred to on page 44 as "Harford motion."

surance of his love, that I may not deny him his glory by calling in questeon his wonderful love to me the chief of sinners: and for growth in grace.
So also at night he made me pretty earnest with him for healing and
amending of my backslidings for a new heart. And the rather for the sweet
incouragement giuen me in his ordinances by his word; telling me of his
omnipotency, and that as god can so he will do for those that take hold of
his power to do for them. So I do endeavour and desire to do, and long for
thy salvation Lord, let not my hope make ashamed, effect for me all that
I need seeing thou art able, my greatest request is that I may glorify thee
by making thee my daly trust. I find this impossible with me, but with thee
all things are possible.

I found many vain things in the former part of the day and much dead-
heartedness before noon. but afternoon god in some measure helping me
to hear himself speak things that concerned mee. Lord let me hear and see
and feel thee daly for thou onely art my stay whom I chuse. fail me not,
let not me fail thy expectation.

Heart much gone from god again this day in pride and some pang of   29
passion and inconsiderate words I fear and vain distractions in prayer. God
is nevertheless my refuge to whom I fly in this time of trouble. For my
pupils all came to me this day to desire they might ceas learning Hebrew:
I withstood it with all the reason I could, yet all will not satisfy them. I
suspect the bottom is they look to commence within 2 years; and think (and
some haue bin heard to express so much) that I retard them purposely.
thus am I requited for my love; and thus little fruit of all my prayers and
tears for their good. God made me earnest in pleading with him for help
and hearing in these things for his owne glory. Now I will wait for his
salvation   When will the Lord appear? can his promiss fail? certainly
it cannot   Lord increase my faith.

I am ashamed of my pride which stil again prevails, when god marvel-   30.
ously assists me in dispute or discourse. Ah sinful heart! Is this thy requital
of all the Lord benefits   Is this the fruit of his chastizing the and letting
the be buffeted with temptations arising from thy owne ignorance to
humble thee. In the distress of my soul and in sorrow's and temptations I
fly unto him and he entertains me, and do I thus requite him? God appear'd somewhat in inclining the spirit of my pupils to the study of Hebrew
as I had pray'd that god would do, who can turn the heart as rivers of
water. but my sins come in to stop mercys Lord forgiue and heal.

God hath somewhat endeared my heart to himself made himself sweet   31
unto me by leaving me to distress of conscience and strong conflicts about
doubtfull matters in practise: the principal whereof I think was no duty of

mine, but rather would have bin ridiculous to meddle. So that I know no rule of god but my heart desireth conformity thereto. And now this morning (thursday) the desires of my soul are after the Lord Jesus, that I may haue him for my resting place. I am exceeding affraid of losing him: sith I find multiplicity of occasions (that hinder much my studys) do expose me to think too much time spent in his service; my studys and my pupils are in danger to draw my affections from christ. And troubles that I meet with otherwise to abate my trouble for sin. Against these things I set my face. Lord giue grace that I may in all things honour the and not provoke and sin against thee; my eyes are to the and my hope is in thy help onely.

what I feared I found this day my heart exceeding proud before meeting at Boston: in time of meeting strong conflicts I had and temptations to giue way to my sloutfull frame and distracting perturbances of mind. in a word a piece of hel I found in my heart.   god helpt me over it somewhat to savour his rich grace which was held out in the sermon.   o blessed be his name who lifteth me out of the lowest hel.

2
3 }

God caused me to taste an Emptiness in my studys, and to make my *soul* desire himself   *God left me to speak somewhat in the welcoming of friends with my mother which my heart did not speak and therefore I desire to mourn before God for my falseness and hypocrisy*. I hope the Lord hath in some degree answered my long desires in graunting me of late a spirit of fear least I should lose christ (though mixt with unbeleif under which I desire to mourn) and of longing desires that I might, that I might daly haue communion with him and rest my soul in his bosom that I might make him my life; though I cannot attain it; but my heart is aboue all things deceitful, soon weary of following after god, apt to question the trueth of his promises at least my intrest in them, because such bent of spirit to rest in the creature to savour that more than god, and so little humiliation for such things as this, I cannot mourn bitterly for my grieving the spirit of christ Jesus. Why therefore I see the more necessity to fly onely to the blood of sprinkling, and to trust barely to his mercy and faithfulness, who hath once and again ingaged them and himself to me and particularly twice in the Lords supper; and that is the fruit that I find by that ordinance, vizt. that my faith is revived and supported amidst discouragements, by seeing the Lord hath given me his christ and his grace therein, and my unfaithfulness cannot make the faith of god of none effect; nor my want of sorrow for sin undoe me for I haue come to him for that grace in that ordinance; shal I perish for want of that which I come to him for? I lose my desires after this grace.. yea but I came and daly come to christ, for a heart to desire him, and shall that be my bain? is there no balm in Gilead for these plague sores?

How glorious and precious are the words of my Lord Jesus to me when he opens my eys now but a little to see the loue and grace that breaths out of his heart to his people in giving himself to be fed on by them?

Deliver me our Lord from a spirit of impenitent security for I am not able to see the poison of my sin, and to loath my self for it: deliver from slouthfulness and sensuality: for all these I know wil be my bain this day, if thou prevent not. The good Lord forgiue and pardon and help though I be not prepar'd according to the preparation of the sanctuary. God did help me to lay hould of christ as my prophet priest and King   whole christ I se need off, when as he exhibited himself to me in the sacrament. I find a stupid hard heart that cannot feel the sting of sin, and therefore I am unworthy of him.   yea but god has exalted this christ (whom he now giues me) to be a prince and a Saviour to giue repentance and remission of sins, therefore I come to him the rather because destitute of all grace in my self. I was exercis'd with strong strugglings in my spirit to make out to my self that God has instituted this ordinance as a seal that he giues christ to every beleeving receiver as really as bread and wine: I can see that 'tis a representation of what christ has done for us, I cannot see so clearly that it sealeth the present gift of christ, as that it puts us in remembrance that christ has thus giv'n himself to us if upon examination we find that we belong to him. I longed to hear some means to help me over this simple, and because I could not therefore I was affraid I should partake unworthily. In some measure god helpt me to see christ giuing himself to me and to close with him whom god hath made wisdom because I am nothing but blindness and folly. I come to him the rather because I want eyes to see his glory and to understand his mysterys. Lord Jesus be my teacher! ah sinful wretch Laden with iniquity I find pride again and again prevail this day.   god be merciful to the chief of sinners; I feelt at one short him that frame of not seeing a glory in the blessed estate of the world to come, a stem of that root of amazing wickedness of my heart.   why therefore I fly   therefore. I cry to the Lord Jesus to save me.   when shall thy salvation, Lord, appear according to thy promiss and my saviours purchase? Blessed be god for Jesus christ and for the hopes which I haue in him, o that my hopes might always be in him alone!

Munday and tuesday. I found iniquity, and apostacy of spirit from god so apt to creep in amidst my multitudinous occasions, too much bent of spirit to my studys and pupils, and affections dying toward god; that I am exceedingly affraid of my owne heart therefore I desire to be instant with god for pardon and succour and I cast my soul into the armes of his fatherly

sabbath
day
4

{ 5
{ 6

protection; Lord let me be inabled daly to loue thee and follow hard after thee.

I am still exceedingly affraid of my whoarish heart and weary and asham'd of it. Lord! hast thou giv'n grace to dy for the to many of thy servants (their hearts lov'd thee so dearly) and shal not I haue or obtain grace to liue upon thee and unto thee; never any had more caus. I would ev'n lay violent hands upon this grace of god which I want: now is my gathering time, Lord, let me not be fruitless. myne eys and hands and tast are witnesses to me that thou hast giv'n me thy christ though (to my shame) my spot be not the spot of thy children, why give me grace to love him according to thy word.

The lord thus help's me over my doubts concerning the Sacrament   If the onely end of it were to represent unto us what christ hath actually done for us: then when god call's me to discern the Lords body (that so I may not receiv unworthily) the meaning is either I am to beleiv that christ was made an offering for sin; and so may a Devil do; or a hypocrite may do it and so be a worthy partaker: or els I am bound to beleiv that christ hath after this manner giv'n himself to me heretofore, which beleiving, I discern the Lords body and am ergo a worthy receiver; but I may beleiv this (as some doe) and be mistaken, and so beleiving an untrueth makes me a worthy partaker. Therefore I am to beleiv. (if neither of the other suffice) that christ is just thus giv'n to me, to discern by faith god giving him now to me as surely as he gives me this bread and wine. Again if god did not now really give and offer christ, how could I by unbeleif be guilty of the body and blood of christ of dispizing it and spilling it on the ground,? for it may be I never had christ giv'n me really (that is made mine) heretofore.

Dies ult:/ Blessed be god the father of my Lord Jesus that hath brought me so near another Sabbath. Lord make it a day of rest to my troubled soul! I am at a strait concerning my answer to Harford motion; [22] I am indifferent to engage or not, to look toward England or not, if I could be clear in gods call. Friends advice cannot satisfy my conscience. who but God can now be my counseller? but god I am daly forsaking and dishonouring, by my pride and whoarish affections. I find not onely Emptines and dissatisfaction but difficulty in my study's yet my deceitful heart is prone to fly from one flower to another to quiet it self, and not go to god. I come to him to seek pardon of these sins, and supply of these wants, but with how little affection though seemingly earnest; my judgment tells me what reason there is I thould walk otherwise, but I cannot inforce my self to

[22] See note 21.

melting sorrow for the dishonour I do to god by my sin; I am affraid of it
and disquieted with it till god giue me some hopes of his acceptance, but I
cannot get my heart humbled under it; ah Lord why dost thou leav me to
a spirit of errour? why doest thou harden my heart from thy fear? Outward wants at least the fear of them disquiets me, or would do: but I dare
not let them make impression, nor be earnest with god for supply of them,
lest, my desires thereof should exceed my desires of sanctifying grace. Behold Lord my pitiful case: remember thou art my father though I be a rebellious child: ah put a childlike spirit into me that I may make thee onely
my trust. say to my soul it is not in vain to seek thee.

I found much deadness and little brokeness of heart for my sins this day,   11
and some risings of Atheistic thoughts I find that the clearest Arguments
that can be cannot perswade my heart to beleiv the being of a god, if god
do not let the beams of his glory shine into it. I found also unbeleif, and
discouragement my hands hang down and knees are feeble and I am ready
to say 'tis in vain to seek sanctifying grace of god: or at least to think I am
hardly dealt with that my prayers haue been so long shut out from acceptance. Ah Lord! hear the groans of thy poor prisoner, who desires to re-
nounce all for thee and thy christ, and caus me not to err from thy wayes
nor harden my heart. When Bashan Languisheth and Carmel &c. now do
thou arise according to thy promiss. why should sathan, and my own unbelieving heart insult over me saying where is thy god? Let me find grace
to giue thee glory.

Tuesday at night god helpt me to cast my self upon himself as my onely   13
support with somewhat more affection, and taking hold of his promises
than ordinary. my fear then was least I should more long after other things
than deliverance from sin. Unbeleif is apt to prevail in my heart in that god
so long refuseth to hear my prayer for my self and for others; yet I desire
with patience to wait the Lords time submitting to his wil as best.

Lecture day./ I bless God for taking off my heart in any measure from   14
my studys, and for making me see any need and haue any desire to find
him in his ordinances. And that I found any awakening presence of his
there. though for a great part of the while my heart was marvelous stupid
considering that god put me in mind of my never enough bewayled grievings of his spirit by a fleshly heart both off, old, and at presente. when I
came home I set my self to seek the Lord. for my whoardoms are many,
and my grievings of christs spirit thereby, but my repentance small; my
pride (as at this day) frequent, but my humiliation and soking sorrow seldom; for which caus I am affraid. I confes't these things with aggravation before the Lord, and he gaue me somewhat more affection; but yet

I fall short, and haue attained nothing compared to my sins. And thats the reason I attain not redemption because not weary and heavy laden with my sin as committed against god.

friday   I find my usuall distempers pride and inordinate affection to the creature, weariness of gods worship, vain distractions in dutys, and manifold iniquitys breaking in like a flood. Lord in thy multitude of mercys pardon, heal, and take not thy holy spirit though grieved from me

This hath bin a day of great temptation; though the Lord hath not let me be very much distracted; yet so awakened as solemly to fly to the throne of grace and cry with all my might for preservation out of temptation or at least that I might not be forsaken so as to sin against god wittingly by any vain words unsutable to the day. The reason of this temptation was the being here of a stranger what we could not but intertain both in the Hall and our chamber. The Lord hear'd my poor broken disordered chatterings, and in som measure kept my self, and hept me to administer to others occasion of religious discours. Yet I find so much of that plague of pride which my soul hateth: of a heart that cannot desire great lettings out of christs love to me such as some times I haue felt which I dreadfully fear, such aptness to be weary of seeking god in his ordinances, to lose sence of my misery, of unbeleif: that I haue caus to sit downe astonied that such means produce so small effects in so long time. That which is wanting cannot be numbred; yet god is with me in his ordinances touching my heart in some measure with these things; oh that I could feel my owne emptiness so as not to know what to do without pardon and supply: as it was in the exigency above mentioned. Lord I bow the knees of my poor pining soul unto thy self my father, who art rich in mercy, compassionating oppressed sinners, that thou would seal to me pardon, and thy love and giue healing for thy faithfulness for thy glory, for thy son, for thy everlasting love sake.

I felt fears and misgivings about my good estate. yet much pride got head in me; and presently the Lord let loos upon me some scruples of conscience which put me in fear least I went cross to gods will, and this to abase me.

25   I found besides much prevalency of pride, a heart apt to run after mirth and recreation. God assisted me much in my study. And now shall I again take his name in vain in this approaching sabbath, which I find I haue too too much accustomed to, and look't at it as a light matter, not watch't against it as I should haue done; especially grieving god by vain thoughts. Lord forgiue this trespass, and giue repentance for and deliverance from this with all other abominations.

I haue found much of gods presence in his ordinances this day: much   26
stirring my heart in the forenoon by such sutable trueths. Concerning the
good ground and the effects of the word therein: yet at noon my filthy vile
heart could find room for pride: and vain thought after noon in the beginning of the sermon exceedingly prevail'd whereupon when Mr. Mitchel
came to uses of strong consolation from gods constancy in his loue I begin to question gods love to me; and that one crevis of hope that hath
chered my soul so long when other evidences fail'd, god plucks that from
mee too, at least suffereth unbeleef to darken it vizt my renewed acts of
closing with christ at his supper. and other times. when I look upon my
vile ungrateful impenitent whorish heart I am ashamed to think that god
should love or owne me. I abhor my self o Lord for these renewed incurable distempers. I could even take vengeance of my cursed heart that
is so deceitful and desparately wicked in impenitent departure from god.
Nevertheless through the riches of thy grace I am imboldned to ask peace
with god and pardon and communion with God (which my heart breaths
after, for that is my life) and a new heart after thy owne wil. Hide not
(my father) thy face from me, lest I be like one of those that go down to
the pit, lest I sink in discouragement and say 'tis a vain thing to seek the
Lord.

There was an Artillery sermon[23] here a munday. I found my heart se-   27
cretly weary of the ordinance, and hankering after my studys or other occasions: a frame which I was exceedingly affraid of, and desire greatly to
loath my self for. But Lord it puts me to a stand to think what mean's this
that my heart is worst in appearance when I most earnestly strive but the
day before for deliverance from these evils. How long oh Lord wilt thou
be angry with my prayers? and withold mercy from me. I feel a heart
that hath no power to cleav to thee ready to fall utterly from thee. I fly, I
cry I cast my soul o Lord into thy armes. Lusts and creatures shall not
haue my heart through thy grace, noe I set them all at a defyance. thee I
desire to chuse, o leav me not! let iniquity never never, never haue dominion over me. forgiue I beseech thee my trespasses and cause thy face
to shine upon me, and so shall I be saved.

4th day. works of iniquity prevail against me; I am unworthy to lift   28
up mine eys to heaven, becaus proud and vain and forgetful of god. yet
verily thou art my father, as thou givest me ground of incouragement; becaus I find a daly restlesness under sin committed without renew'd repentance; my soul is breathing after god with my spirit within me I de-

---

[23] The sermon which was delivered at the annual election of officers in the Ancient
and Honorable Artillery Company.

sire him; Emptiness are all things else; god cleareth up to me his calling of me, and causing me sundry times to come to his son and close with him upon gospel termes especially thrice at the Lords supper; and if called then justify'd, and then I shall be sanctify'd. Lord realize this grace of thine unto me, for my unbeleiving heart can scarce reach to make these things real to me.

October 2   On the sabbath I found both bodily spirits and spiritual desires much dead and down the wind, yet the Lord kept me desiring of him. he is the onely soul satisfying good.

3   Munday/ I found an unsavoury abominable spirit amidst godly persons and godly discours; and abundance of pride of the favour and acceptance I find with man. Outgoing of heart I fear too much after discours and dispute, and time mispent therein. for these things I desire to abase and abhor my self; ah Lord hide not thy face, harden not my heart from thy fear.

4   Again some prevailings of pride, and imprudence in not redeeming opportunitys of profitable discours for my owne furtherance. I find a heart so hard that cannot be affected or humbled for such things a slight spirit in performance of holy dutys that hanker's after my studys through unbeleef, which finding my self so unable to make work off, and that indeed I can do nothing, I am loath to rely upon and therefore to seek earnestly gods assistance. o Lord I beseech thee forgiue and saue me from all these abominations, be thou my strength.

5   Mr Sims[24] preaching at watertown upon this point a people that are near to god, may be not sought out but forsaken et contra; I haue not found more of the presence of god awakening and affecting me (even unto tears) for my sins, particularly of slighting and weariness of gods precious ordinances, unprofitableness under them, &c. my own iniquitys were so touch't; together with gods gradual departure from my self, and from this whole country, that took deep impression upon me. I was partly unwilling to goe to this lecture but company drew me on; and I bless god that he forsakes not me though I be forsaking him. the desire of my soul is that the fruit of such meetings with god might continue. but woe is me I find the same weariness of spiritual dutys the same carnal, formal, heart at a private meeting the same night, together with pride.

On friday I besought the Lord on purpose. for help in my studys finding some very difficult knot, and through mercy he help't me to se through it in some measure. the desire of my soul is after the Lord, but I find vain

[24] Zechariah Symmes, a graduate of Cambridge University, was pastor of the church at Charlestown from 1635 to 1671.

distractions so pestering me that I cannot seek him to purpose; pride prevail's also, and some mispence of time I fear. Lord forgiue and heal for
thy mercy sake

Sabbath. Innumerable evils compass me about   vain thoughts on gods
day in his ordinances break in upon me like a flood. I am less than the least
good thought. yet the evening before and this morning in prayer at the
private meeting and in the hall god assisted me extraordinarily with his
spirit in prayer; especially at our private meeting melting my heart before
him.

I was sadly assaulted after noon when I heard of gods trueth with doubt-
ing whether ever word of the scripture were infallible because of possi-
bility of mistakes in the writings and because of the points in the Hebrew,
and the various readings in the text and margent. for these things (o
Lord) I crave pardon, and bring my blind eys and vile heart to thee for
healing. thou art he whom my soul desires to enjoy, whose wil I desire to
know and do o teach me thy wayes   thou art my god

I went through much business, and found god above my strength carrying me through intricacys two hard for me, at my earnest intreaty. But
an unthankful heart I haue; pride and a frothy light unsavoury spirit, and
so much spiritual cooling of affection toward god and his ordinances, little
desire off opportunity to meditate off or hear god speak to me, all which
are a burthen to me; and I am most affraid off a spirit so drown'd in my
studys that savours not gods presence or ordinances. deliver me deliver me,
O my father, from such iniquitys, pardon me for thy mercy sake, and
faithfulness, heal my backslidings by converting grace, and love me freely,
for thy love is better than wine. caus me really to se at once thy love and
my own vileness.

Wednesday. Afore lecture the Lord much assisted my studys   At meet-   12
ing I found as my natural spirits faint so my spiritual affections low, and
heart little stird. yet after I came home I set my self seriously to cry to
heaven for pardon and deliverance especially from a heart that cares not
for, that is weary of gods ordinances. It is a death to think of being left off
gods spirit in his ordinances and left to set light by them. But Jehovah thou
art my trust be thou my life.

friday morning. I had some fears in my spirit about the immutability of   14
gods love in case I should fall away from him; but the Lord did in some
measure clear the absolute stability thereof from the scripture. In the forenoon I met with great difficultys in my studys and my strength failed me, I
besought the Lord for his help, and though in the forenoon I could make
nothing off it, yet afternoon I was exceedingly helped and my work made

marvelous easy. But ah! ungrateful heart, I take gods name in vain in my nearest approaches to him, and prophane his ordinances for this I am not able to stand before him. God brought to my mind in special (being at a private meeting) my want of love and dutifulness to my parents, which I beg'd pardon of

15   And the very next morning news is brought me of my fathers death. whereupon I set my self to confess before the Lord my sins against him in want of naturall affections to, and sympathy with my afflicted parents, in my not prizing them and their life which god hath graciously continued so long. My great request is for pardon of all former sins, and present deliverance from a stupid frame of spirit unsensible of gods visitation and my owne loss in losing such friend. my humble supplication is to the Lord to sanctify his hand to me and all of us whom it concerns and to become a father of the fatherless and husband to the widdow. my Father dyed the first of october.

16   On the sabbath I was earnest with the Lord not to giue me over unto a spirit senseless of his afflicting providence, and to forgiue all my sin in that kind; in not being so instant with god as I ought to haue bin for my fathers like &c. ut supra. I was much exercised with scruples of conscience in some old cases (*as Mister Mildmay's sword and Major Sedwick's*[25] *son*) but I desired to lay down my soul at christs foot, and to know his wil that I might obey it. Lord lead and guid thou me in a right path. God discover'd that unto me, that makes me fear I haue faln far short of my duty in making use of christs merit to plead for sanctifying grace. withold it not from me for that caus, o my god!

18   Tuesday morning. *I found the same cause of crying earnestly to the Lord and of grace for a right spirit under God's afflicting hand that I might not be secretly glad that my father was gone. I have given God much business this day and done much for others but I have no confidence nor satisfaction in mine own doings but my soul longs for the Lord   When wilt thou come unto me   Pardon I beseech thee my pride my stirring affections my taking of thy name in vain in giving of thanks and seize at my soul with thy goodness. The last night some filthiness in a vile dream escaped me for which I loathe myself and desire to abase myself before my God   O Lord deliver me from the power of that evil one.*

19
20   Wednesday. I was at Watertown lecture where the Lord awakned me with the sence of that monstrous vileness of my heart that cannot desire heaven and communion with christ; and stird me up that night and the next morning and night to cry and strive earnestly with god for redemp-

[25] Robert Sedgwick was one of the founders of the Artillery Company and a leading figure in the colony.

tion, giving me some weak measure of faith to beleev that my seeking should not always be in vain.

The latter part of the week I spent in preparing to preach at Chalstown.   24
In my private studys the Lord much assisted me; But I spent near three days in the same, whereas one day at Martins Vinyard sufficed me, Like those that gathered manna, he that gathered much had nothing over, and he that gathered little had no lack. When I came in publick the Lord much assisted me, and emboldned me, and when I came to close application much inlarged me; As I return'd home that night through some feared neglects of my duty, I had some ecclyps of my comfort in god (who is my onely portion, whom I am not worthy to name) but god remov'd in some measure those feares and how sweet was his returns to my soul? my heart blesseth him that he takes any cours to make himself precious to me at any time; woe is me! that it is so often otherwise through a spirit of whoardoms, ah Lord remember not inquitys against me for thy tender mercy sake, remove pride and apostacy of heart far from me.

On the 2d day at night in my sleep I dream'd of the approach of the great and dreadful day of judgment; and was thereby exceedingly awakned in spirit (as I thought) to follow god with teares and crys until he gaue me some hopes of his gracious good wil toward me.

The next day I found my self unable to make any work of it at my   25
studys. pride prevailing.

Wednesday. My iniquitys are extream pride which I am weary of as a   26
body of death and ashamed off before god; and a mind ful of distractions in holy dutys; neglect of improvement of opportunity of discours for advantage in my studys: negligence in not redeeming the opportunity to send a letter to Harford according to promiss. I know not what to do but my eys are to thy son Jesus christ. hide not thy face from me; my soul cleaveth after thee o Jehovah; I deserv to be confounded by the; but let mercy pleas thee, thou art my god; thou wilt be my redeemer.

On the last day I went to Concord where I preach't out of Isaiah 57. 1.   29
I had but extream short time. some few thoughts I had had of it before, but not resolved to take it till sunset the Last day night; gods assistance was here the more remarkable.

Tuesday I drive the time of my return so long till it was so late they would not suffer me. wednesday. It began to snow exceedingly so that I saw god locking me up there to wait his pleasure; it continued snowing til it was knee deep, so that I knew not when I was likely to return: then I recall'd how in all the journeys of that nature I haue taken these many years god has cros't me remarkably, the Lord shew me his mind in it. I set my self seriously to seek the Lord, and he heard me and caused it to rain on thursday and that night so as abated the snow to the ankles thereby giuing me a season of returning on friday. what shal I render to the Lord for all his benefits.

In this my journey I haue met with sundry trials and temptations. As 1st feares concerning my owne estate when I feel such a wicked heart as cannot love and desire communion with god, as can be weary of gods service, and be eager to be at other studys: this is an amazing consideration to me, and I know not what to do; but the Lord he awakens me to find some need of him by other providences that set me a seeking him with fear least any iniquity should separate me from him. *As in point* of *their not reading any part of God's word in public duties at Mister Bulkeley's*,[26] *I questioned exceeding whether I were not bound in conscience to speak something to him of it The scruple still remains Lord* assail *it.* be thou the strength of my heart and my portion for ever: for I find an end of all other perfection. Vanity of vanities all is vanity and vexation of spirit.

Saturday at night I was importuned to go preach at Roxbury because the Elders were both ill. I did so, and preacht out of the same text I had done at concord. the Lord assisting me more than formerly when I preach't the same.

Munday and tuesday the Lord mightily facilitated my studys and prosper'd me therein: yet takes off my affections from them, so that my soul longs for Jehovah. Behold I see an end of all perfection; vexation in studys when most succesful; in pupils, o Lord be thou my portion.

9   wednesday. I feel such distractions in holy dutys, such deadness of heart at lecture, such pride in divine assistance and in my own notions, even then when I haue bin taught to haue no confidence in the flesh, a pang of worldly desires amidst hearing the word, that I am ashamed to lift up my face to heaven: father forgiue or else I perish, Oh hide not thy face which is my life from me.

I think I haue found of late more ful purposing to follow the lord universally, and more longings after the returns of his spirit to my soul after communion with him than formerly, especially since the discovery of my want of love to and desires after God at Concord. yet abundance of pride prevails and some whoarish affections, which I am ashamed of before god. On the last day the Lord awakned me to seek him earnestly both for pardon and grace against the evils of my owne heart, and for mercy to this society.

But above all my vileness breakes forth again whilest I am hearing the

[26] Peter Bulkeley, one of the founders of Concord, was minister of the church there.

word. An Atheistic irreverent frame seizeth upon me; and whilest God is bidding me see his glory I cannot see it; vile and unworthy conceptions concerning god come into my mind. I cannot desire heaven because 'tis a place where I shall see and wonder at and acknowledge the glory of god for ever; But I rather desire a heaven where I might be doing for god than onely thinking and gazing on his excellency. Blind mind! Carnal heart! I am affraid, ashamed, heavy laden under such cursed frames of heart, as ever and anon beset me. My soul groans my body faints o Lord whilest I pray and cry to the for pardon and redemption. Is there no baulm in Gilead? no physician there? Look down and see my plague sores which I spread before thee my saviour; wounds and old putrifyd sores which provoke the Lord, stink in his nosthrils, and poison the peace and comfort of my own soul. Behold I am vile, when thou showest me my face I abhor my self. who can bring a clean thing out of filthiness, I was conceived bred brought up in sin. O redeem from these devouring Lyons the hopeless shiftless soul that thou hast purchased.! I deserv to be the stepping-stone of thy wrath why behold I lay my self at the foot of mercy as low as thou wouldst have me, confessing my self the cheeif of sinners. Lord what wouldst thou haue me to doe? shew me thy wil, and bow my heart to obey it, and I haue what I do desire. O lift up the light of thy countenance upon me and hear my prayer; shut it not out for ever.

Munday. when I come in company affections dead toward god, and too much savouring the creature. also pride; and aptness to be ensnared by my tongue hereupon fears and misgivings but the Lord in mercy scattered them.

Tuesday morning. I found special assistance in prayer. the Lord causing my heart to love him. I fear least I should griev him in not obeying all his known wil, but for this I wil trust him, who alone wil work all my works in me and for me. 15

Wednesday morning. I had bin much perplexed with the ill carriage of one of my pupils, and had some thoughts of admonishing him openly, I besought the Lord before hand and he guided me to act in a fairer way; and ishued my trouble to my good satisfaction. But o pride pride, and outwandrings of heart from my resting place. Lord lay them not to my charge; for thou art the desire of my soul hide not thy face from me. 16

yesterday I was in a doubt whether I should goe to watertown lecture or not because of multiplicity of business; I went nevertheless. And this day through Gods assistance I haue done as much as I used to doe in two dayes Thursday 17

Friday morning the Lord let in some comfort in that, though I be sinful and impotent unto any thing that is good yet he hath made christ righteousness and strength to me and accepts me through him. which was evidenced to me by my longings and reachings of heart after the Lord not finding satisfaction any where else: And in my desiring the promoting of Gods glory, that he may be advanced by my self and many others. How can I loue the Lord or his glory except he haue lov'd me; and if he haue so done he wil ever do the same.

Dies ult. The Lord's Supper being nigh: I am affraid at the thoughts of it; And wel I may having a heart so vastly unsutable to be at any time near god, More fit to ly lowest in Hel that I might be farthest from him. For upon search I find, (yea I haue dayly found, though not sufficiently felt) 1: A blind mind, often questeoning the most Palpable truth's and unable to clear them to my self though I would never so fain. As whether God be: whither the scriptures be his word, and that alone without corruption, at least through errour crept into the text. How it appear's that the Lords supper is a seal as wel as a sign; which doubt I was sorely assaulted and buffeted with the last Lord's supper. Whither christ's purchase were of all the good I need, or onely of pardon of sin and deliverance from wrath; other things being freely giv'n of god without any purchase, though disposed by christ; this doubt I am scarce able to extricate my self from by the word of god as yet, though I exceedingly desire it and do grope after the light. And so for light in my daly actions. Fearful shakings frequently assail me, and I would stand fast upon the word of god but I can find no foot-hold. My knowledge and faith is thus assaulted by the powers of darkness when I should be nearest God to receiv much good from him; thus pittifully am I made to stagger instead of coming to him. 2: Carnal security and hardness of heart all sence of want and misery gone, when I approach to the fountain of mercy, especially in hearing the word. 3. whoarish affections apt to rest in the bosom of creatures. 4. Want of dear love to the Lord Jesus and his appearing, a Brutish swinish heart that cannot savour Heavenly things and spiritual ordinances. 5. Pride. 6. Slouth. 7 Vain distractions in holy dutys. 8. want of sence and sorrow for my Fathers death, o Lord forgiue! 9. want of heart to seek Gods glory 10. Unfruitfulness under so many means of grace, and daly visitations of gods spirit; who having the like would not bring forth more fruit? I hope the Lord hath of late giv'n me a little ground against inordinate affection to the creatures, and made my soul to breath somewhat more after himself; which I sought him for in such opportunitys as these heretofore.

I came to the Lord supper under the guilt of all these iniquitys, and with the plague of a hard heart little affected or sensible of all this sin and misery considering it was so great. But I saw the more need of a saviour to deliver me from the guilt of so fearful abominations and to save me from the power. I saw need of a priest to reconcile me to god. and yet no less need of a prophet to teach, and of a King to rule me, to bring all my lusts into subjection, such a christ I desired and still desire to close with, and no other christ I would haue. God helpt me in some measure against my blindness of mind, and doubts concerning the doctrin of god which I besought him for and was affraid of; and sent me out of his presence. I hope somewhat incouraged in the grace which he had made mine by his gift and my receiving yet afternoon I was assayled with feares in reference to my unsensibleness under gods visitation in my fathers death and I feared least there should be some root of bitterness that I were not willing to part with, unsearched out. But I know none, Lord search and try me, and make me upright before thee. yea blessed be thy name for Jesus christ in whom thou wilt redeem my soul from distruction, and crown me with loving kindness and tender mercys, Lord I beleiv help my unbeleif.

Munday. my spirit was much sunk within me being conscious to my own weakness and fearful to check some disorder in the scholars, I besought the Lord and he helpt me against my fears, and assisted me to it in such manner, as I was proud of it, O wretched worm that I am! O body of death! do I thus requite the Lord? The Lord made me earnest with him for pardon and more grace.

wednesday was a day of publick humiliation. I desir'd to bless god (so far as I know my owne heart). that as he had giv'n me christ to be bread of life to me, so now he put an opportunity into my hand to sue for supply of my great spiritual wants. but I could not with all I could do get a melting broken heart this day; but I had a hard heart besides all other plagues to spread before the lord: Lord look down in mercy and let not my soul sinking iniquitys be my ruin. I know not what to do: harden not my heart from thy fear, nor this day pass away without some wound to my sin, and some quickening to the graces of thy spirit in me, for the lords sake that I may enjoy the, thee for my portion, and glorify the onely, continually. be graciously reconciled to the cheif of sinners in thy welbeloved for thy favour is better than life, help me to prize it constantly, for so brutish am I that of my self I cannot. forgiue in mercy the pride and hardness, and vain thoughts of this day. ₂

I am ashamed and know not what to do because I find such fearful prevailing ₂₅
of pride the next day after I have betook myself most solemnly to the Lord to deliver me therefrom. I may groan with the Israelite and say my bondage is rather

increased when I begin to stir for deliverance   O Lord why hast thou hardened my heart from thy fear or sufferest me to err from thy ways   O return to me for thy servant sake thou art mine only hope./I was quite puzzled this day and the greatest part of it could do just nothing.

27)
29∫

Since the fast day till now I haue scarcely bin wel, nor am yet. On the sabbath I preached out of Psalms 81. Israel would none of me &c. Gods spirit did not enlarge my heart as sometime it hath done; when I come to speak in Cambridge, I haue twice found god shutting up my heart; so that I am ashamed to think that I marr the word of god I meddle with. yet pride fearfully assailed me the next day, and deadness of affections god-ward. I am affraid least the Lord for these things should take his holy spirit from, and giue me to my owne hearts lust. o Lord why dost thou leav me to err from thy wayes and harden my heart from thy fear? How long shall I liue in thy world to dishonour thee? O pardon my iniquity for thy favour is my life, and shine upon me with thy grace and I shall be saved!

30

The Lord helps my soul to long somewhat for himself and to fear the losing of his spirit which I grieve and to seek earnestly his assistance in my study which I have found these two days though almost discouraged with difficulty yet carried on by God's power and strength and the rather because tis his work that I am about. But O my many sins Lord forsake me not

The last day I found so much trouble of the spleen, as forced me to leav study. I preacht notwithstanding at charlstown the Lord much assisting me and imboldning. The church sent to me after sermon, and I could not get off without engaging to preach once a month til March equinox. I partak't of the Lord's supper at Charlstown   the Lord helpt me to desire and close with whole christ. yet my affections were but low. And since I find pride monstrously prevail. o Lord why is sin strongest when I come to christ Jesus to subdue it? Is there no plaster that can heal this sore?   thou art my hope, o be thou myne help; deliver me from my owne heart.

On the lecture day I heard awakening truths. we were call'd upon to a serious hearty mourning for sin. the want of this is the reason we liue without or with so little assurance of gods favour. I could not get my heart then affected with sin; no I had no incouragement to set my self to it; so blockish and stupid am I that a little meditation wil take no impression upon me. yet the Lord gaue me a sweet and supporting meditation amidst the pittiful impotency of my owne I think on friday morning.

Gods visiting hand has now pluckt away 4 from us in a few days   Goodmen Bancroft, Wilcock; Briggan, Cane.[27] all brethren of our church.

[27] Roger Bancroft, William Wilcock, Thomas Brigham, and Christopher Cane were

I went to the graue of the last upon the last day, and there I had some serious thoughts about this token of the heat of gods great anger, and my own sin kindling thereof. I came home and set my self seriously to meditate, and call over the sins of my whole life by a Catalogue. And the Lord was pleased to set in, and in some measure break my heart for them. showing me my desert to be kickt out of this world because I haue not had naturall affections to my natural father, but requited him and all my governours evil for good: and to be shut out of the world to come, because I haue rebell'd against and dishonour'd and disregarded my heavenly father, been a viper in his bosom where he has nourished me. And especially because I am the man who sin to death god['s] precious servants, a sinner that destroy much good, that drive away god from the place and society where I liue, and pull down wrath; yea I haue sin'd to death the Lord Jesus, this most affected me that I haue crucify'd the Lord of glory, and as if that had not been enough I am daly grieving and wounding his heart afresh, yet so blockish am I (O monstrous hardness!) that I can go up and down the world little afflicted and grieved with it.

And o then what need haue I of a saviour whom god holds out to me this morning publickly as the onely way of favour with god. O let him be mine! let thy favour be mine o Lord! pardon my sin that I may not come into condemnation; neither visit my sins upon others. rather let thy hand be upon me o Lord for my sins than upon others for my sake, I haue done wickedly, but as for these poor sheep whom thou afflictest, what haue they done; especially what haue my pupils done whom thou hast blasted and scattered, and one thou hast taken away for my sin in too eager seeking their good with neglect of communion with my god. if they haue sinned, yet Lord forgive them they know not what they do. but I haue known sin, and tasted thy sweetness, seen thy glory, yet despiz'd thee. For this cause my soul fails within me sometimes but o let thy mercy in christ Jesus speedily prevent me. shew thy glory in pardoning the chief of sinners all his inquitys. I haue not layd to heart the beginnings of thy visitation, when 2 were taken away from us, and two from the church; so the Lord rents away 2 more church members, and come again with sickness into the college. Lord pardon my sin which helps forward this wrath and turn to us in tender mercy (o thou my god whom my soul desires), for I haue no hope no portion but thy free mercy in christ Jesus and thy love which is better then life.

Munday at night being the preparation to the fast I set my self to pray,

---

all members of the church in Cambridge and freemen of the colony. Bancroft and Brigham had served as selectmen and in other town offices.

but for confusion and distraction of spirit could make nothing of it. Finding my stomack very weak and my body faint I was bold to eat a hearty supper; afterward the Lord shew'd me I had done evil, and against the nature of a fast, and that I had been heretofore too much tainted with that too much indulgency to my appetite, especially on the Lords days, under pretence of the trouble which I find by an empty stomack. Lord I bless thee for discovery of any evil. after this the Lord something assisted me in meditation and prayer the same night.

The next day perceiving how the tokens of gods displeasure were upon me many wayes, in crossing my hopes and scattering my pupils being angry at my prayers, and also refusing to giue me victory over my corruptions, yea suffering them to prevail most after solemn seeking of deliverance at his hand. I desired to humble my self under the mighty hand of god and to acknowledge my iniquitys all of them, and the desire of my soul was after the Lords face and favour, for it is my life;. Brother Danforth[28] exercising afternoon and declaring the causes that he found of lying low and being abased before god, so hit my sins one after another, with such affection, that I know that ever my heart melted into such plenty of teares so long together, at the sight of all my iniquitys; security and thence arizing. Atheism unbeleef, want of love to the Lord Jesus who loved me in the midst of my misery, slouthfulness, want of love to the people of god, little good done little receiv'd: that night in prayer the Lord incouraged me that I should be heard.

Next morning God shew'd me a great reason why he refuseth to answer my petitions is because I haue not been deeply sensible of my own utter unworthyness; this I desire more to see. yet o the wearines and secret hankering after an end of such services! O the pride and sensuality of this day again! Lord I deserv non-attention to my cry, but rather to be given into myne iniquitys hand, I deserv thy displeasure and wrath, but o deliver me from both for thou art all my portion, if thou fayl me wo is me for all is gone. but thou art a god that pardonest iniquity and healest it because mercy in christ Jesus pleaseth thee, therefore haue I hope.

God hath prosper'd me this day in every thing I set my hand unto, both in my own studys and in my pupils diligence. abundance of work he has carryd me through o blessed be his name; but I haue no confidence in my doings   my soul longs after gods grace through christ Jesus.

[28] This may have been Thomas Danforth, then treasurer of Harvard College and later Deputy-Governor of Massachusetts; or it may have been Samuel Danforth, who graduated from Harvard in 1643 and worked with John Eliot as missionary to the Indians.

Friday morning I could not make out to myself the devine authority of Mark and Luke's gospel because they were no Apostles. I desired to be humbled for my owne blindness, and betook my self to the giver of wisdom, for understanding to know his word and his wil. Pride still giues me the foil notwithstanding all my striving against it.

Saturday. I am affraid least I should fall short through unbeleif: yet I   17 know on whom I haue trusted.

I discover this day slouth again in not using betimes to seek the Lord.   18 o prophane heart to whom god is not worth abiding a little hardship for. A confused spirit distracted me in private prayer though not in the perfomance of publick dutys. Carnal security, that Laodicean frame that I am rich and feel no present pinching wants when I come to gods ordinances, that I haue lost the sence of sin and desire after christ for my self and desire him onely or cheefly for others; the thoughts of this dismayeth me. When I come to be desired to repeat the sermon publickly, being assisted pretty wel to perform it pride seizeth on me, for which presently in prayer I judge and desire to loath my self before god. Lord teach me once to think lowly of my own doings. After this it was told me that some sayd I made the sermon better than it was preached; here I excused and put from me such a thing.   the Lord sets this upon my spirit and layes me at his foot under the guilt and acknowledgement of hypocrisy.   o clense me my god from falshood and all guil; wash me from my guilt I beseech thee and redeem from the power of my iniquitys for thou art my god.   overcome my unbeleef and all my evil with thy goodness.

Tuesday at night I was at a private meeting where I found the Lord   20 awakening my heart by a sermon repeated out of that text because of the abounding of iniquity the love of many shall wax could. abundance of iniquity is therefore in my heart whose loue to christ is waxt so could.

Thursday I spent in study to prepare for the next day which was a day of private humiliation in our colledge. I found the Lord somewhat affecting my heart upon the fast day morning, but afterward again heart very hard, and little sence of my owne wants and woes, stirrings of pride I think even then when I should haue been onely self vile. yet toward the evening when I came to speak my self out of 1 samuel 7. 3 the Lord mightily flowed in upon my spirit, both affecting and emboldning my owne heart, and furnishing me both with variety of matter and heart breaking expressions, and did even wonder at the divine assistance for I had had little time to study and scarce time to read over what I had writ. the like enlargement I found in prayer so that I admired at gods lifting me aboue my self and the rather becaus he hath twice shut up my heart before when I came to speak before the students. I was affraid of a storm of pride after this and I begged of the Lord power against it which in some measure he graunted blessed o blessed for ever be his name.

Yet the next morning I was miserably foiled with pride, in dispute, which I was suddenly abashed with and ashamed off within my self, and am so the rather because I had bin near god in my morning meditation desiring to put away Baalim and Ashtaroth and to serv the Lord onely. O Ephraim thy goodness is like the morning dew! Lord pardon. hide not thy face from me. my soul longs for Jehovah. I find no rest for the sole of my foot els where.

this night speaking at the meeting the Lord discover'd to me that I had oft times been too impetuous and peremptory in my prayers For the good of others. god wil haue earnest yet humble petitioners.

25   Mr Mitchel preacht from 1 John.17. his use was for trial whither the grace of god belong to us yea or no; Art thou in christ, dost thou beleev. here god in some measure cleared my intrest in christ from my faith, which is indeed the main evidence I haue. yet I find it hard to make this real. can god love such a proud, carnal, secure, hardhearted wretch as nothing wil mend? yes for christs merits he can and doth. Lord I beleiv, help my unbeleif.

Afternoon I found god awakening me from that doctrin the death of the righteous unlamented is a forunner of evil to come. O Lord my security I am shut up and cannot come forth. I am ashamed to think of what opportunitys I enjoy and what pains god takes with me yet my ould sores stil running: he is oft awaking me in his ordinances, and in his sanctuary I haue another sight of things, but o my goodness is as the morning dew. I am affraid of my senselesness of my fathers death. also of my secure hard heart the Last sacrament I was at at charlstown, and this last fast; for these I begg remission. Lord I hoped to haue bin a stander in the gap, but thou wilt make me see that I am a maker of breaches by my security and a hastener on of wrath.

27   2d.3d day./ Boldness to transgress the colledge law in speaking Eng-
28   lish[29] I am guilty of and so off distracted wandrings in prayr and giuing of thanks. is this my reverent serving and seeking the Lord. So pride on tuesday. for which cause I am even ashamed heavenly father to look up. God awakned me this evening in the hall at Exposition, with fear because I could not feel that groaning after the resurrection which the Apostle speaketh of Romans. 8. oh the stupid security and sensuality thats daly creeping into

[29] The laws of the college at this time required the members to converse in Latin.

my heart. o when Lord shall I be delivered! return o Lord with thy pleasant bewty to me and make thy loue a real thing to me for the Lords sake.

I am ashamed before the Lord to think of such a prophane spirit of Esau which I find to haue my mind running after my breakfast whilest I was reading the word of god. O what need of a redeeming kinsman; of a brazen serpent to fly to when stung with fiery serpents! o Lord be reconciled to me, and turn from thy displeasure; behold I take hold of thy strength according to thy word, let me make peace with thee, as thou promisest, not for my faith but for thy faithfulness and son his sake.

Friday morning the Lord gaue me a more liuely meditation than ordinary, both helping me to judge and abase my self and yet to beleiv his grace.

Jan. 1. On the Lords day I was at charlstown and preach't there and received the sacrament. wo is me! what a blockish secure heart I find that cannot be sensible of my wants, though before hand I know them, and see they are such are ready to swallow me up every day. Lord withdraw not the blessing of thy ordinance from me therefore, for whole christ I long for. yea but sometimes I find no power to long after christ, but I come to thee to work in me. both to wil and to do. Lord I abhor my self for my pride for stirrings of fleshly lusts: Behold I am as a beast before thee and I am even weary of my self and off the world by reason of my sinful self. yet I am unfit for heven, because unfit for earth; and therefore fit for hel and no other place. yet Lord if thou wilt own and accept and bless such a wretch and honour thy self by me, shal not Eternity sound forth thy praises for such grace? do it then Lord for thy name sake!

On the lecture day I was affraid of the Lords hand being again strech't out to destroy us, Gest being dangerously ill at the time.

Jan. 8. On the sabbath and before it I found god awakening with fears lest I should never haue mourned aright for sin, vizt. as it grieveth and wrongeth god. And verily I feel little of that spirit, what cause to be for ever ashamed that I haue enjoyed such means and such a hard heart to this day. but I hope there hath been some degree of that sorrow, Lord encreas it. God further awakned me by his word from 57. Isaiah. 1 for my security and all those fearful evils arising therefrom, which I therefore bemoaned my self off before the Lord. as being sensible that my sins are ready to swallow me up and tis impossible for me to keep near god except the Lord put forth his almighty power. I am affraid of my own evil heart yea I feel the plague upon me that wil be my ruin unless the Lord prevent, which I trust he wil do. O forgiue the weariness of thy service this day and my whoarish heart. I fly onely to the blood of a saviour for attonement and there I rest, Lord cast thou not off my soul, be not far from me.

9   munday I found pride monstrously prevailing, for which I am ashamed and know not what to do. *I found also some scruples of conscience whether it be my duty to speak to some to* see *whether there be no snow drifted in over some studies.* I know not what my duty is. I am foolish and blind and sinful, and therefore exceeding affraid lest any thing should separate me from my god, either for the present or for ever; for my soul chuseth god for my portion and longs for him both now and for ever. therefore I earnestly beg pardon of sin and the grace of his spirit for time to come that I may once cease to rebell against him. ah Lord pitty me for thy name sake. I disputed for Ramus in the Distribution of the 2d part of Logick against Richardson[30]   my Arguments found such acceptation with the seniours (though contrary to their former apprehensions) that pride prevailed upon me poor fool that knew nothing as I ought to know.

12   Thursday. I find not onely pride mightily prevailing but also, a slouthful, sensual, secure heart that can secretly hanker after other bestowing of my time than in seeking god and reading his word, when god giveth me opportunity. this makes me affraid of my own sincerity. Oh! I find such a bottomless gulf of vileness in my heart that I am ready to fear lest there be no trueth in such a prophahe deceitful heart. for this cause I fly and with the outstretched desires of my soul I cry to my heavenly father for pardon and redemption.

The next day morning and evening the Lord awakened me by the fear of that evil which I yesterday discovered in my self to seek him earnestly. Because I find my self not able to desire communion with him in any ordinance, if he leav me to the woful prophaness of my own heart.

15   On the sabbath day I found prevailings of pride, and weariness of taking pains in seeking god. yet the Lord did awaken me to seek him earnestly though not without reluctancy, partly through slouth partly through unbeleif. I am saying in my heart what profit wil come to me by seeking god; I pray and come to sacraments &c. and find no good; hence I am secretly loath to come often to such ordinances, my heart is in a bad frame and I cannot get it out: When I bethink my self how god brought me out of the

[30] The logic of Petrus Ramus was followed by all New England theologians. Alexander Richardson, a tutor at Queen's College, Cambridge, was the author of a popular commentary on Ramus. Wigglesworth seems to have been arguing that Ramus' original organization of the subject was better than the slight modification of Richardson. See Perry Miller, *The New England Mind: The Seventeenth Century* (New York, 1939), chapter v.

miery clay and horrible pit, and purchased me by the blood of his son to do him service; o me thinks were I any other then a beast, why I should not refuse to suffer the torments of hel all my dayes upon earth if he would so haue me to glorify him: but now the painful performance of any spiritual duty is too much to undergo cheerfully for his sake. god and christ are not worth taking an hours pains for. Lord what shal I say? thou hast redeemed me, led me through a howling wilderness to humble me, and there spoken to my heart, visited me oft in thy ordinances, yet I haue lost my affections to the (or else I never had them) thou hast smitten me and the tokens of thy displeasure are upon me, yet I haue not been reclaimed. neither the fire of thy love nor the furnace of gentle affliction haue purged away my dross? Lord what wilt thou do with me,? hast thou no plaister that wil cure these wounds? Oh remember thy covenant, and bowels of mercy, and son christ Jesus lose not thy glory in pardoning the cheif of sinners for my unworthyness.

$\left.\begin{array}{l}16 \\ 17 \\ 18\end{array}\right\}$

2d & 3d day I found abundance of pride. conceitedness of my own notions ah! wretched creature who shal deliver me from this body of death. yet the 4th day morning I had a sweet reviving meditation   god perswaded my heart, that notwithstanding my unspeakable vileness, yet if christs righteousness might be accounted mine, I should be acceptable to god and beloved; and also he cleared to me that he had given christ to me and drawn me to him; ergo Therefore my soul findeth sweetness in god   oh that I might go away and sin no more against him. Get from me unbeleef   it is not in vain to seek him for this also.

$\left.\begin{array}{l}19 \\ 20\end{array}\right\}$

That 4th day with the 2 next I enjoyed more sweet affectionate melting meetings with god than ordinary. yet when god is nearest to me I am wandring farthest from him. so much pride as is entrapping me every where that I cannot get victory over; such outgoing of affections after my study and impatiency in that I make no more riddance of business; such fretting against others dulness to learn Lord I deserv to be forsaken by thee, as I haue forsaken thee and gone awhoaring, I am affraid of losing thee who art my onely resting place, my hearts content. Ah Lord! what worthless things are all my own services   my two main petitions this morning were that I might enjoy thee, and glorify thee; but loe to dishonour thee I ceas not, I can do no action for thee; but how much against thee, and therefore I deserv to lose thee. Lord I ly down in my shame and misery at thy footstool.

on the sabbath day God touched my very plague sores vizt these things kept me from coming to christ and finding the good I want in him. 1st sencelesness of my owne need of him. 2ly Ignorance of christ his worth

22

3ly Quieting my heart with other things before I find him 4ly the enmity of my heart against him. 5ly slouthful negligence in seeking after him. The great evil that I conflicted with again this day was a greater desire of others finding christ than of my own. I find that amazing iniquity at the feeling whereof my soul is even filled with confusion many times I care not for more communion with christ. And as for conformity to him though I long after it yet I cannot beleev that I shall obtain it. these evils I was groaning under and conflicting with this day. I am worn out with study wel nigh; yet god reneweth my strength.

27   Friday night. God awakens my heart to cry after him; seeing that even hypocrites may tast of the joys of the world to come, and suffer persecution for christ, and I sometimes find such a monster of iniquity in my self that I can see nor tast no excellency in communion with god, how seldom is it that I having a living sight of him? this Lord I groan under as my greatest plague.

I found my heart very dead and unable to be affected with gods grace in the Sacrament yet fear'd and strive against it least I should prophane gods ordinance. God helpt me nevertheless I hope with truth of desires after whole christ, and so to close with him   The Lord awakened me again at night with report that one of my pupils had broke his arm, which was not true, yet sanctify'd by god to awaken me at that time   my soul blesseth god when I find it otherwise.

30   My soul longeth for the Lord, not onely for pardon from him, when my sins beset me roundabout and the tokens of gods displeasure are upon me and the country, but also for his sweet soul satisfying presence which is the life of my heart, Lord pardon my sin and heal my backslidings and love me freely.

February 1/

The desire of my soul is that I could see God in christ Jesus to be the cheef of 10000s, and walk all the day long in the light of his countenance. I am affraid of losing him whom my soul loveth, by losing my love to him. I find it not possible of my self to maintain it. sin estrangeth my heart, and opens a dore to unbeleif, creature comforts poison my affections; my love becomes a lust to other things. Though my plague sores be every day breaking forth to gods dishonour, and ready to separate my soul from god (which makes me long for deliverance from them, and for continuance of gods sweet soul satisfying presence) yet such is my unbeleef and slouth, and over-valewing of other studys, that I cannot with willingness take time and paines to cry mightily to god, until he reveal himself and love clearly to me and subdue my iniquitys. I am most unsensible of my present necessity of christ, when nearest to him in publick ordinances, and do what I can my desires are rather carried that others may find him that are wholy without him, than my self. Lord help me for I am imprisoned by my iniquitys and cannot come forth. Let it be possible with thee to uphold by thy right hand that so I may follow hard after thee. O take away all iniquity; my slouth and unbeleif especially; Father teach me thy wil and let me obey it in love with delight for thy name sake which thou hast begun to glorify in the cheef of sinners.

The Lord pleas'd after this to give me some measure of confidence in him and communion with him in prayer ☞ tis not in vain to seek him.

Yet oh how oft haue I provoked him this week, by pride by, apostatizing   4
in myne affections to other things? I find my desires to my ordinary studys one while, and to the study of points of divinity another while ready to grow to a lust. O how impossible is it to keep up my affections to god and communion with him, and to seek him with living desires and without weariness in all his ordinances! yet thou Lord art my choice; and there is no sin which I fear like to a heart that cares not for thee; wherefore my soul and all that is within me blesseth thee, for that thou hast so often made me feel the emptiness of all other things. O thou unchangeable god! make me stil seek, and let me find enough in thy self to satisfy me. Thee I must haue what ever it cost me, and therefore thy whole wil I am resolved to do, let earth and hel combine against me; teach me thy statutes, and giue me strength to obey them. I haue no confidence in my self; I feel that every day that's ready to carry my soul for ever from god: but all my sufficiency is off thee who hast promised a new heart to me. Let it be possible with thee, holy Father, to create me anew to good works. nothing is impossible with thee, pardon and subdue my iniquitys. help me once at last to obey thy commandments out of love, and accept me in what I do for the Lords sake.

Mr Oakes in his use[31] advizing to see spiritual plagues to be the greatest   sabbath
evil in the world out of Ephesians 1. 3.   5

I was awakned with fear of myne estate because me thought I could not se more evil in sinning the least sin than in hel torments. ah Lord! to thee alone I fly in Jesus christ, that thou wouldst help me to se sin the

[31] Urian Oakes graduated from Harvard in 1649 and became a teaching fellow there. He went to England in 1654 and did not return until 1671, when he became pastor of the church in Cambridge. From 1675 until his death in 1681 he was also President of Harvard College. The phrase "in his use" refers to the section of the sermon known as the "use," in which the preacher drew practical applications from the doctrines which he had expounded in the earlier part of the sermon.

greatest evil as it wrongs and offends thee. I am asham'd that I haue now stood these 3 years as a shrub in thine orchard, and made so little improvement of christ, that I may questeon whither I haue him, or no.

I had also sore conflict this day in my spirit about buckling to do more for christ than I haue done by reproveing lightness and mad mirth on Sabbath Evenings and by visitings. Lord thou onely art able to make every way of thine easy, all my confidence is in thee. God further discover'd to me the vileness of my sin in want of naturall affections, and in being asham'd as it were of my poor kindred.

6}
8}

ah Lord I can sin against thee by pride, and cooling of affection by a common heart, and immoderate anger and swelling against others miscarriages, but I cannot mourn for sin indeed. And this want of a broken heart makes me fear and suspect my self. yet Lord I wil cleav to thee; thou hast made me thine owne by purchase, o make me like christ Jesus; and work in me all that thou requirest. for thou onely art my refuge and helper, let me obtain a heart to glorify thee before I go hence and be no more.

Want of a broken heart for sins of infirmity, to account them a body of death more bitter than death; that hath bin my exercise, and I think daly fear this week. my heart is hard and what through multitude of business and failing of bodily strength, I cannot strive mightily with the Lord for a contrite spirit. And now this last day morning, though I were abroad at charlestown lecture yesterday and there awakned with the opposition which I felt against something which I knew not whither a duty or no; although my soul was loosened from all creature comforts finding the vanity and tormenting emptines of them; yet I found this morning an indisposition to seek god in prayer to purpose, through woful slouth and unbeleef, and longing to be at some other work. Although my soul long after the Lord, yet I cannot willingly take pains in seeking him, till he be found. The vileness of my heart that's fil'd with enmity against god is unspeakable; yet 'tis possible with thee Lord to subject me to thy wil ah! remember thy promiss, though shame and confusion be my portion, yet to thee Lord belong multitudes of mercy, be thou faithful in thy covenant, for thyne own name sake. rescue me from the power of all my iniquitys, and accept me in christ Jesus.

12

God gaue me some comfortable perswasions of his grace begun in me from sundry markes given out of John.1. 17. 1. In that god in the day of his power came with the offers of his grace to me in particular. 2ly in that he made christ sweet and precious in some measure, not onely at my first receiving him but daly he is my heart contentment my soul satisfying good.

3ly In that he answerd all my objections both at first conversion and often since, at the Lords supper rather making arguments of them. 4ly In that the awful power of gods commandment to beleiv came so with autority to my heart, that I durst not but beleiv. what shall I render to the Lord for all his grace and love? Lord I do beleiv, help my unbeleif; I desire to obey all thy commandments, subdue my rebellious will that I may become thy willing subject, and strengthen me to do thee more and better service.

yet I found much pride, outgoings of affection after creatures, peevishness at others unteachableness and perversness whereby I fear I dishonoured god. for these causes I am ashamed to lift up my face to heaven. 13

I am exceedingly affraid this morning, because I can feel so little evil in sins of infirmity; therefore my soul cryeth to the god of my hopes. 14

wednesday morning upon the obstinate untowardness of some of my pupils in refusing to read Hebrew, god brings to mind and ashameth me of my own perversness herefore both to my naturall parents and Achademical: and also I see that this is the spirit and I fear if the Lord prevent not wil be the ruin of the whole country A spirit of unbridled licentiousness. Lord in mercy heal, or I know not what wil become of New England. 15

Friday I was at a private fast kept by the church. where my principal request was to be delivered from spiritual plagues. I did especially conflict with this day hardness of heart (that cannot grive for that I am grieving god by my smaller sins of infirmity) weariness of gods ordinances and desire of an end, unsettledness of heart and failing of my resolution to follow the Lord fully, a heart that is ready to halt between 2 opinions whither I should do the whole wil of god or no, and this I find stirring upon such times as these the wretched frame of my heart upon such blessed dayes makes me affraid when they come. ah Lord deliver my soul out of the mouth of those lusts that are ready to destroy me; set me at liberty for thy name sake, that I may continually glorify the and mourn for my falling short. 17

On the last day I was taken with inconsiderate untruth in my words which God made me ashamed of before him

On the sabbath I preach't at Cambridge out of 81. *Psalms*. 10.ii. I was much surprized with fear before I began; I besought the Lord earnestly for his assistance and he assisted me and strengthen'd me to the work, so that I was not at all abash't or very little when it came to. Since, I am very ill in my body and know not how I shall be able to study. O what a sinful miserable world live I in, Lord grant I may glorify thee in it, and enjoy thee. 18

26   The next sabbath I preach't at Charlestown being (through mercy) prettily recovered of my former ilnes. At the Sacrament the Lord made me in some measure ashamed of the declensions and apostacys of my heart from god, unto a loos frame of self love and creature-exalting (and *carnal lusts as much*) he helpt me to close with whole christ as prophet preist and King, such a christ I desire and none other. Woe is me that there is a spirit of backsliding in me so soon after god hath been near me

27   I find pride, unbeleeving discouragement joyn'd with pride in reference to my pupils, some doubts about casting all aside of that nature   one class is at least yet resolv against it by gods grace. Above all Lord keep me from a carnal heart, and from taking up my rest in the creature.

F. March. 1

On the lecture day the Lord discover'd to me more of the vileness of my whoarish departures from god and inordinate taking content in the creature and the secret weariness of my heart of that spiritual duty of meditation, when the Lord was giving me sweet communion with himself on the last sabbath day at night. My soul even trembles at the horribleness of those my iniquitys so fearfully aggravated. and I am sensible of my desert and therefore affraid that the Lord should forsake me, and leav me to my lusts, and sins and to dishonour him.

Ah! moreover I cannot seek after future settlement without carnal aimes. Lord that it might be possible with the (all things I know are possible) to pardon me the cheef of sinners, and to heal my backslidings O when shall it once be. Say amen to my groanings after thee, and strengthen me with strength in my soul that I may follow hard after thee. And let me see and enjoy, and rest satisfy'd with thee and thy love as a full portion: subdue this untowardness and unconquerable enmity of heart against thy will, that I may become one of thy willing people rejoycing to work righteousness and to endeavour that others may do so to.

5   On the sabbath day morning I was somewhat affraid lest my soul never rested in christ, or took up satisfaction in christ alone. the Lord helpt me over these fears by reading in Mr shepard's sound Beleever,[32] in that 1: I dayly war and wrestle against a heart that is resting any where but in christ. 2ly because my wandrings make for my further establishment and closer cleaving to christ; God sendeth vexation in the creature and maketh me to seek and find more abundant sweetness in himself. so that I concluded christ was mine, and all spiritual blessings in him according to Mr Oakes

---

[32] Thomas Shepard, one of the most famous of the early New England divines, was minister of the church at Cambridge from 1636 until his death in 1649.

his text out of Ephesians 1.3. yet I found so much unbeleef that I could not make it real to me, and so much sensuality that I could not se the glory of this priviledge and rejoyce in it, as we were exhorted. I found also a multitude of vayn thoughts, and neglected to go and reprove some carnal mirth in the lowest Chamber til it was too late, which I pray god to pardon.

Stil I find my whoarish affections forsaking the sweet fountain, setting   6
light by him, and digging broken cisterns. Therefore the Lord goeth on to smite me, in the stubborness of my pupils after all the warnings given them; And I goe on frowardly; being quite overcome of anger ·when they came not to recite, almost out of patience. thus Lord I am that sinner that destroy's much good by adding sin to sin. I ly down in my shame before the, and acknowledge that the Lord is righteous; but O let not thy own work fall to ground, but turn their hearts, o Lord, who can do it as thou turnest the rivers of water.

I was much perplexed in mind with many thoughts to and fro, about   7
leaving the colledge, one while ready to resolv upon it almost, and quite another way; and I know not what to do, how to liue here and keep a good conscience because my hands are bound in point of reforming disorders; my owne weakness and pupils froward negligence in the Hebrew stil much exercise me. yet for all this trouble god hath bin with me in my personal studys; for this day I began and finished all that part of my synopsis which treats about method. Blessed be god whose strength is perfected in weakness.

Pride estrangement of heart from God and outgoing after the creature with   8
some stirrings of carnal lusts this day which I am afraid of Notwithstanding   cant
get my heart so to loathe as I would   O Lord leave me not to return with the sow
to her wallowing in the mire   Let me not live rather than live in my lusts

The thursday I went to Boston and from thens to Mr Butlers[33] he being married. There I found my heart secretly departing from god hankering after the creature. but at Boston lecture and at a private meeting at Mr Butlers god did in some measure awaken and recal my straying affections

The sabbath I found god awakening and quickening my heart to cry to   12
him for more sanctifying grace seing it cometh onely by christ; and the reason why I haue so little I was tould is from security, slouth and fulness of self or the creature. The sabbath evening and the next day I was much distressed in conscience, seing a stable dore of Mr Mitchels beat to and fro

[33] Probably John Butler of Boston, said to have been a physician, who later moved to Connecticut, or Henry Butler of Dorchester, who graduated from Harvard in 1651, taught for a while in Dorchester and subsequently settled in England as a nonconformist minister.

with the wind, whither, I should out of duty shut it or not; no temptations perplex me so sorely as such like, when I am not clear concerning my duty

my fear is lest my wil should blind reason. this made me seriously and solemly cry to heaven for light to my mind, and grace to obey with chearfulness all gods wil. And still I cry, Lord leav me not to er from thy ways

subdue the enmity of my heart in tender mercy for thy name sake: pitty my poor fainting decaying body. my strength and my heart even fayl within me by these temptations and the difficulty of my studys (which by distraction I cannot attend freely) and the continued perversness of my pupils. Lord hear me, for I haue none but thee.

I adore the wisdom of god who can let a proud and carnally secure heart blood in the right vein. By the forementioned temptation he hath made me with earnest and humble addresses to the throne of grace cry for light to my mind and grace to my heart to do his wil. ah Lord leav me not to er from thy wayes. my heart trembleth to think of any way of wickedness. Lord search me and try me (as far I know my heart I do desire it) and if there be any guil o turn me from it! when shall all thy paths be paths of pleasure to me?

sabbath

On the sabbath I was stil afflicted with the like temptations which made me with my soul powred out cry to heaven. It was some support unto me amidst these temptations to read in Mr Goodwins book how christ Jesus is a high priest that knowes with bowels of compassion to pitty his poor tempted people, for himself also was tempted for that end.

22

Now I am ashamed before the Lord of my pride and common carnally secure frame so soon after I haue had such experience of my owne blindness and christ Jesus his compassion in giving me some respit. ah sinful heart! dost thou thus requite the Lord. Lord Jesus thy blood to cleanse me I fly to, and thy spirit to renew me. O when shall I obtain it! *Deliver me O Lord from carnal lusts These make me afraid when I feel my spirit so prone to close with them.*

This week I studied natural Phylosophy with Sir Ambros Juniour.[34] I found the Lord so extraordinarily assisting me above and beyond my own folly in quickness of invention and reasoning; that in stead of admiring my god I found my self very prone to admire my self; And so like a wretch I turn grace into wantoness. ah Lord! I loath my self for this: I am even weary and groan to thee under this body of death: I haue such a clog at my foot that I cannot lift up my feet to run the wayes of thy com-

---

[34] Nehemiah Ambrose (called Junior because there was another, older student, Joshua Ambrose, in the same class at Harvard) graduated in 1653, went to England and became minister at Kirkby in Lancashire.

mandments. Lord forgiue, Lord for thy mercy sake subdue my iniquitys.

Next sabbath I preach't at charlestown. The Lord in some measure help't me to fight against my lusts especially that of carnal departure of heart from god after the creature; *which I found myself ensnared with by provision that the sixth day morning I had a motion of marriage made to me which was sent as a message from Mister Buckley My heart was too much taken with it. Notwithstanding at the sacrament the Lord helped me to close with Christ Jesus as prophet priest and king with some affection. On the* 2d *day again I was ready to be gone awhoring after other loves and to cool in my love to God though at a private meeting the 2d day at night the Lord awakened me and helped me to loath myself and so again on the lecture day*

On the lecture day the Lord set in with his word to convince and affect for that spirit of distance from god which is gaining ground of me, and I cannot prevail against it. I set my self to think off those things and to seek the Lord with my soul powred out in prayer for deliverance from this body of death; and that he would not let christ Jesus be a dry christ unto me that I should close with him in ordinances and sacraments for life, and yet find none. the Lord much affected my heart and somewhat strengthened me in prayer. Lord let it be possible with thy majesty to hear me and help for thy name sake 29

Friday. I stil feel my carnality of heart (that seeks after sensual contentment and cannot find satisfaction in god) prevalent. I strive against it, yet it prevails, and I am ever and anon ceasing to strive; For this caus I might wel make tears my meet, because the Lord answer's me not, but ah my heart is hard and cannot mourn after the Lord.

sabbath/ The wise god who knoweth how to tame and take down proud and wanton hearts, suffereth me to be sorely buffeted with the like temptation as formerly about seeing some dores blow to and fro with the wind in some danger to break, as I think; I cannot tel whether it were my duty to giue them some hint that owe them. When I think 'tis a common thing, and that 'tis impossible but that the owners should haue oft seen them in that case, and heard them blow to and fro, and that it is but a trivial matter, and that I haue given a hint to one that dwels in the hous, and he maketh light of it; and that it would rather be a seeming to check others mindlesness of their own affairs, and lastly that there may be special reasons for it that I know not; why the case seemeth clear that 'tis not my duty. yet I am sorely affraid I should regard iniquity in my heart, and god upon this ecclypseth the sweet beam's of his love, he hideth his face and I am troubled. I would not for all the world be a worker of any one iniquity. He hideth his face justly from a wretch that could not prize it, but am bold April 2 to wax wanton and proud when I haue it. But Lord pitty my languishing soul and feeble spirits and frail body ready to fail under the blow of thy hand if thou rebuke.

3   *I still find pride and whorish departure from God prevail though not in the particular of marriage as before but Lord make me watchful Lord make me spiritual by all thy dispensations.*

7   Thursday/ Ah Lord! teares of blood cannot wash away the guilt of this dayes horrible pride and spiritual whoardoms in departing from my god. Ah my god! wil neither the sight of my own pittiful blindnes, nor thy hiding of thy face for these things of late, nor all ordinances nor providences nor sacraments nor nothing do me god? But my plague sores run day and night, and I find no healing   oh my father, why hidest thou thy self away and takest thy holy spirit from me? Lord I am vile, I abhor my self that bundle of folly and madness, who forsake the fountain of living waters, and follow after vanity and lies.   oh how unfit am I to bear thy name and declare thy trueth to others? I can do nothing but pride and self do surprize me.   ah wretch! for this caus I loath my self; Lord do not thou forsake me utterly.   if christ be mine why am I thus?

9   On the friday I began to prepare for preaching at charlestown out of Luke 5. 32. my time was short, and strength small. I was somewhat sensible of more want of a plerophory in what I writ than ordinarily I am. On the sabbath day I was ill, and ill provided in committing to memory what I had; yet the Lord gaue me much gracious assistance according to my earnest desire blessed be his name. *I found myself very apt to be ensnared by pride and self admiration and setting forth myself before others though the Lord helped me to strive against it.*

10   I find my self this day in comming home scarce able to think a good thought; but apt to rove after vanity and to trouble my self with future contrivances for which I haue oft smarted already and by which my god has been provoked, Lord I beseech the to forgiue in mercy and to heal my backslidings   o let me enjoy a portion in thy sweet favour, thats my life   make it more precious to me, that my self may see and savour the things I preach.

Wednesday morning I meditated of the vanity of the favour of men to take off my heart from seeking it or pleasing my self with it. At even my earnest sute to the Lord was to spiritualize my affections, and let me grow in that grace especially.

16   I preacht here at Cambridge the next sabbath. I was much at a loss about the explication of my text Acts 5. 31.   what was meant by a prince and a saviour; it troubled me much on sabbath day morning to distinguish

aright between those two. yet god graciously helpt me over the difficulty in some good measure, and my own unpreparedness. I hope god enabled me at the sacrament to be somewhat sensible of my many spiritual plagues and to desire and close with a whole christ both as my prince and saviour. But it is a sad thing to feel a carnal heart never more prevalent then immediately after I haue come groaning to the Lord Jesus in such a solemn ordinance for redemption from it. Ah Lord! what the very next morning? wilt thou not be Pacifyd toward me but set my old whoardoms of heart in departing from thee in the light of thy countenance? shall it be impossible for me to obtain from thee spiritualized affections. to lay up my happiness in things above? Behold I ly down in my impotency and shame and unworthyness, deserving that thy spirit should take no pleasure in me. righteous art thou o Lord and faithful in thy covenant. Lord shew me what keep's thy spirit at a distance from me.

The next sabbath I preach't at Charlestown.   23

A Relation off our Voyage to New Haven and return.

On the tuesday I set sail toward New Haven afternoon, And arrived at   25 the place desined the next Saturday sev'night at night, twelve dayes. In which long and tedious Navigation putting in at no port, my pacience was much exercised, especially considering that it was such a busy time with me. The Lord taught me in some measure to labour after submission to his will, and to wait his good pleasure, though I found my heart marvellous impetuous and impatient in my desires. when we pas't by Elsabeth Islands it was evening and we steer'd on our cours that night: the next morning was rainy and foggy, and we could see no land though we suspected we were near it and by sounding found it so. we thought it had bin Point Judith and were running upon the broad side of Block Island, not imagining it possible to be come so much to seaward; yet we perceived shoar and stood off, and immediately god scattered the fog so that we saw clearly it was Block-Island when as before we knew not what Land it might be. speedily the fogg fell again, so that when we came up toward Fishers Island we feared to fall foul either of that or els off Plumm Island and those other that are on the left hand more to seaward. Here again mark the Finger of God clearing our way by causing the sunn to shine forth in its strength when we were in a strait. Again when we came near Newhaven we were quite befogg'd and knew not when we were come even with it, yet again I pray'd and it pleased God to scatter the fogg and give us a clear afternoon to get in. When we were in some danger in this voyage, it pleased god to withdraw the light of his countenance from me, so that I prayd Lord spare me that I may recover my strength before I go hence and be no more. And Loe! I am spared blessed be the name of my god; why o Lord, my petition is shew me thy salvation. The Lord hath marvelously appear'd in answering my prayers this voyage.

When I came at New Haven I found such love and respect off all hands, that I was thereby lead to overween of my own worth. In my return I stayd a Fourtnight at Harford. Where I was exercised in combating with diverse temptations and prevailing corruptions of my own. Once being to preach the next day it pleased the Lord to come in more than ordinary to melt my heart with the consideration of my own vileness, and the glorious truth which I was to speak about. Concerning the glory of the saints in heaven.

Coming through the wilderness we were overtaken with a great and dreadful tempest of rain and wind. where I beheld the mighty power of god as wel by land as by sea. For all the trees of the Forrest bowed and bended like a bow over our heads as we rid along and divers we heard fall; and about 40 I suppose we see in our way that were newly blown down. I thought how good it was to haue this great god for a mans friend, For loe! how easily he could arm all his creatures against his enemies? And at this time the Lord let in sweet peace and confidence into my heart in the hopes of his favour. For which tast of his sweetness I wil bless his name as Long as I live.

After my return home I found much adoe with a Carnall sensuall heart, that is apt to leav my rest in god, and to seek it in the creature ever and anon. soon gone from spiritual things in my desires and impatient in the pursuit of earthy contentments. Apt to be distracted about those things which are not; and to neglect and be careless in greater matters. The Lord sometimes affects my heart with some shame that I should so dishonour my Fathers hous as to feed upon and be greedy after huskes, when as he hath bread enough for me. That I should promise myself any paradise under the sun when as I have experimentally found all to be vanity and vexation of spirit. That I should mind or desire the Love of the creature, more than take contentment in the love of christ, who loveth me better than any creature can do, and who is more able to do for me what I stand in need of then any, yea then all besides. that I should break my covenant with the Lord Christ and prostitute my soul unto vanity. Ah Lord forgiue my iniquitys for thy name sake for they are very great, and yet let thy love be my portion. When I find my heart so carnal and whoarish, why I am ready to think why the consolations of the holy-ghost which might rais my soul above these vanitys, they are too good for me to pray for. But away unbeleiving heart. The Lords ways are as far above thine, as heaven is above the earth; the grace of god superabound's where sin abounded. O Lord! be thou mine still and then I haue enough! help me to beleiv it.

July
9th

[About a page blank]

After I was come safe home the next day I addrest my self to write to New Haven concerning the whole transaction of this business.[35] when I was doing so there comes to my hand a letter of my mothers declaring that they had propounded a business of the like nature there in my behalf, and that I was now engaged in a sute there, and therefore to see that issued before I look't any further. This report did fill my spirit suddenly with marvellous sorrow and perplexity more then I wel knew how to bear; insomuch that I fear'd least the violence of it should overthrow my bodily health. I was affraid my withdrawing should seem contempt of the party who was of great note and birth and piety, and cast shame upon my friends who had motion'd such a thing as from me (though they had given some occasion and just pretence for my withdrawing) and dishonour upon the name and gospel of my god which I profess. These straits set me upon consideration of my own ways, and mourning for my own pride and self-overweening and rashness &c. And upon meditating much off such things as might stay my heart, and it pleased god to enable me to pray to him and seek him earnestly for to set me at liberty from such thraldom as I had brought my self into through my folly. I knew he could make them to refuse the motion, or however he could bring it to a comfortable issue; I resolved to roll my burden on the Lord and to wait what he would do for me, I hoped in his redeeming mercy and even bles't him for the hopes I had in his goodness before hand. yet I writ endeavouring to undoe what was done. But my letters could not be sent that week. upon the last day comes new's that the business was issued, and the party was to go for England and not to be dispozed of here. At this news my heart was filled with joy and enlarged to bless the Lord with my soul and all that was within me. And I desire I may never forget this answer of prayer, and this mercifull taking of my soul out of trouble

[35] Apparently a decision to get married. Perhaps Wigglesworth had intended to use the preceding blank page to describe a proposal, probably to his cousin, Mary Reyner of Rowley, whom he later married. See below, p. 87

August 5   But ah how apt am I to kick with the heel Jesurun like and lightly to esteem the rock of my salvation? how soon haue I forgotten his wonderful works? A mind distracted with a thousand vanitys sabbath dayes and week days when I should be musing off the things of god But where is my sorrow and bitter mourning for these prophanations of gods ordinances? a thing so grievous to my God. It hath bin some grief to me that I am so unprofitable a servant, that I cannot serv god in my calling aiming at his glory, and doing it as his work. I haue begged this mercy but alas! I cannot attain it, but I lose myself and my love to god amidst my multitude of occasions. My heart is hurried now this way, now that way by divers lusts; one while anxiously sollicitous, another while pleasing my self with this or that creature, this or that project, but ah! where is my walking with god, and rejoycing in the light of his countenance? And now good Lord haue mercy on me! how unfit am I to sanctify a sabbath, with such a carnal heart, such dead and dul affections, such distracting thoughts as posses and fill my mind, such a faint and feeble body? And how much more unfit to partake of a sacrament? I am affraid I shall abuse it: at least get no good by it, But the same carnal, secure, vain sensual, slouthful, proud, unbeleiving, unthankful, unfruitfull frame remain in me still. He also (even the sonns of God) is flesh; this is that which grieveth the Lord at the heart. such an one am I: oh! that I could relent and repent with hearty sorrow. And when shall it be otherwise good Lord! when shall it once be? Thy ordinances are of thyne own appointing and in them thou wilt be sought; and wilt thou not be found? Is it invain to come to sacraments and beleiv on, and feed upon christ as given by thy self? I know it is not invain: though my sins be not yet subdued, though my wounds are yet unhealed. faithful is he who hath promised and will perform it, though I be vile. I feel dayly a spirit of whoardom in the midst of me, a heart revolting from god to the other things. But yet verily Living and dying thou art my hope, o do not fail me utterly; forsake me not o my God; but uphold me by thy right hand in following hard after thee; and let me find that it is not invain to wait upon thee in ways of thy own appointment.

[Page and a half blank]

September 26.

upon examination before the Lord supper I find

1: A loose and common heart that loveth vanity and frothyness.

2. A prophane heart appearing in { Distracting thoughts in holy dutys
                                    wearines of them through
                                    slouth and carnality

3. A proud heart.

4. An unbelieving heart. which questeons Gods love, which cannot wait his time which cannot trust his providence without distracting cares and overwhelming disquietments.

5. An hard heart that cannot be so deeply affected with my sins and spiritual wants, as with my outward troubles this maketh me affraid.

6: A sensual. heart that sometimes can se no glory in heavenly things, no nor in heaven it self.

7ly An unthankful heart

8 A heart full of spiritual whoardoms revolting from the Lord to some vanity [or] other every day

---

At the Lords supper god helpt me to desire, and close with whole christ as prophet priest and King. And though sathan cast objection into my mind because I was no member of this particular church, nor yet recommended hither by Cambridge church; yet I strive against them and said Lord I do beleiv help my unbelief; and o that I might go away and sin no more against so gracious a god so sweet a saviour

I stil find a spirit of pride, and a spirit of whoardom which is restless in roaving after something in the creature; sometimes after this or that study, but I cannot so earnestly desire after prayer, meditation, reading the word this is a body of death and a sorrowful burden to me Lord thou knowest.

DECEMBER

This 2d. day at a private conference, the Lord hath in some measure 4th shew'd me the bewty of holines and fired my heart with desires after it. making me sensible of my vast wants of love to God, of desire after communion with him, off delight in his divine perfections which he hath not for himself alone but for his people, of desire to promote his glory, of sorrow for falling short therein. / especially seing the bewty of an heavenly mind, off affections weaned from this world, in some whom god hath crossed and afflicted, who can rejoyce in their duty attending that onely, let the event be what god wil; this grace I am deeply sensibly [sic] how I want, and earnestly desire of the Lord that he would bestow it upon me too. I bless him that in some little measure he hath granted it off late, though I still want more off the same grace. Lord encreas my humility and faith.

I bless the Lord from my soul for the freedom he hath given me of late from my distracting sorrows; by giving me some measure of submission to his wil, and of faith in his promiss. For I beleiv he wil guide me by his counsel in the weighty busines that troubles me; and then let the Lord do what seemeth him good with me; onely keep me from sin. I bless his name from my soul that he affordeth me a little time and strength to serv him before I go hence and be no more. my god and his service is all that I haue to delight my self in, in this world.

Yet even now when exercised with so sore a trial and besides my ordinary bodily weaknes, with the itch and biles breaking out so as to make me lame; now I say the Lord hides away his face which is all that I haue in the land of the living. my soul oppressed under fears of my estate Lord undertake for me. my afflicting fears rise from some discours at our private meeting to this effect; that hypocrites may go far and tast off the powers of the world to come yet misframe all religion to their own carnal conceptions, desiring a moral felicity and christ to bring them thither, and faith to bring to christ and the word to bring to christ. But they never come to close with god as their last end, vizt, for a principle of life to live to god, and to desire communion with god in subordination to that as the saints do. this touch't me and afflicted me sore, and I am not yet wel resolved of my doubt. yet the good Lord remembered my low and weak estate, whereinto my body began suddenly and sensibly to fall and sent in some support. For 1: I have desired and delighted in, (not heaven or any created excellencys, but) in god himself. who is my hearts contentment.

2ly I do not desire holines for heaven but for the love I bear to god and christ and out of my desire to pleas him. And I should desire it if there were neither hel nor heaven. And I desire universal holines. And it is my very happines to do god some service before I dy; that's all I haue to comfort me against my sorrows. And that is one end why I desire communion with god that I may be made like to him. such a christ pleaseth me best as wil make me holy.

February 15.

My so long intermission of these notes I look upon as a duty neglected, and desire to be humbled for it. This I remember in generall; God hath exercised me 3 wayes since the other was written.

1: By the prevailing of sins, as Pride, which I shall go mourning for to my grave; yet the Lord helps to fight against it. A carnal mind, that is weary and nauseats spiritual conference, and savours vanity and frothines which makes me excessive in the latter, and neglect in the former. Lord redeem my soul from this plague! so also Excess in eating at a feast lately; a snare which I can hardly escape; nor know that I am beyond what is convenient for me til I feel the after inconvenience. I am ashamed and confounded that I should be so brutish. Lord forgive.

ebruary 54

A 2d exercise hath been the distracting scruples of conscience such as formerly. I bless God that hath freed me from them so long

A 3d exercise hath been my weakness. which sure is an affliction many wayes. As first because it exposeth to sin and temptations by day which are too hard for me at some times in some degree. 2ly It exposeth unto *dreams and self pollution by night which my soul abhors and mourns for*. 3ly were it nothing els, but shame, and fear lest it should be judged to arise from wantoness rather than weakness by those that know not the true caus, that were some trial. But 4ly and principally becaus It driveth me to such a strait as I think few were ever in the like. To continue in a single estate, Is both uncomfortable many wayes, and dangerous (as I conceiv) to my life, and exposeth to sin, and contrary to engagement of affections, and Friends expectations, and lyable to the harsh sensure of the world that expecteth the quite contrary: To change my condition endangers to bring me into a pining and loathsom diseas, to a wretched life and miserable death, the beginnings whereof I do already feel at sometimes, and dread more than death; and consequently I fear it would be injurious to another besides my self, whom I least desire to injure.

This hard morsel I haue had to chew upon all the winter; and except the Lord almighty had supported I had been overwhelmed and even distracted with it. For besides all that I haue felt, I had caus to fear wors: nor onely did I fear sorrow but sin also had the danger been onely on the one hand I might haue resolved more easily, but such dangers and inextricable difficultys appear on both hands that I know not which way to turn me. And I may ad to all the rest, that none in these parts have known my affliction, so that all this winter I haue had none to pitty me, none to pray for me, none to counsel, none to comfort me. yea which is yet more than this, I haue even been affraid to pray for my self in this business, that is thus, Affraid to think of my sad condition, because when I haue given way to the thoughts of it, do what I could it was too hard for me and ready to sink me. And hence I have not dared to pray so earnestly and so much as I would for help and health, lest I should be too impetuous in my desires, as formerly I haue been the Lord pardon it.

February/54

But the Lord be magnifyd who hath upheld me by his own hand. These 2 things have mainly upheld me. 1. I knew not whither ever I should live to be put upon these straits; why then should I disquiet my self. 2ly If I should, I did beleiv (and stil do), that the Lord wil guid me in his way, and then let me do my duty and let the Lord do with me what seemeth good to him

Now the spring approaching, I addres my self to write for advice to

Mr Winthrop, Mr Alcock Mr Rogers.[36] In writing the Lord helpt me to do it with plainess and simplicity, declaring the difficultys truly on both sides; and he helpt me to do it without disquieting trouble. I also writ to my cousen[37] dealing plainly with her in the business, what danger I apprehended, wishing her to be advised and to take counsel, that she may know whom she matches with and have no caus to repent her. Blessed be the Lord that hath helpt me thus far. Now my daly and earnest supplication shal be, that God would counsel my counsellers and me by them, that I may attend his will in this great business that is too difficult for me

ebruary/54

18   The Last sabbath and this the Lord hath given me a great measure of assistance in publick beyond my own fears and misgivings of heart: enabling me to declare his trueth plainly, without bawlking any thing that he hath discovered unto me to be a sin of these times and places. I haue gone thorow all the commandments in the discovery of guilt from Romans 3d. 9. Where it hath been my endeavour to meet with the sins of the times, as much as I could, in so short a work. It is my hearty desire to make known the whole counsel of God, and to run thorow the very main things in divinity in a little time: becaus it is somewhat likely that I haue not long to preach. I would do as much for god as I can in a little time. Ah Lord! that I may obtain the assurance of thy love before I go hence and be seen no more; that my soul longs after, and after a real discovery of the glory of heaven that I may be fit and willing to dy. I find pride very prevalent this day: But the Lord helps me to fight against it; and I trust I shall at last overcome it: Good father forgive it, subdue it.

19   Munday. I toyl'd hard and issued little upon the text Deuteronomy 10. 12.

20
21
22   Tuesday. The Lord assisted me very much. so that when I preach't the lecture on wednesday pride was ready to surprize me.

I was much carryd away with too much frothines and love to vanity on thursday and friday having cheerful company in the hous with me. *I found myself much overborn with carnal concupiscence nature being suppressed for I had not had my afflux in 12 nights   Friday night it came again without any dream that I know of. Yet after it I am still inclined to lust   The Lord help me against*

[36] John Winthrop, Jr., son of Governor Winthrop of Massachusetts, and himself one of the leading figures in Connecticut, was a man of wide interests, whose advice on a variety of subjects was much sought after. John Alcock, a nephew of Thomas Hooker, graduated from Harvard in 1646 and practiced medicine, first at Roxbury and later at Boston. John Rogers graduated from Harvard in 1649 and preached at Ipswich for a time but devoted a large proportion of his time to the practice of medicine. He was president of Harvard College from 1683 to 1684, the year of his death.

[37] Mary Reyner of Rowley, whom he later married.

it and against discouragement by it and against temptations of another nature and
disquietments.

I hear off and see such troubles arising here; that my thoughts have
been too hard for me this day about what I shall do. Lord pardon my unseasonable and needless forethoughts, and fit me to attend thy good
pleasure./ Hide not thy face from me, neither lead me into temptation
good Lord.

I have been much troubled with the spleen these divers days And all
I can do wil not get it remov'd. This hath exposed me to temptations of 3
sorts. 1 To too much frothyness and unsavoury discours, finding a necessity of some mirth; readines to be too much addicted thereto. so that I
find no power to attend or love serious and savoury discours. 2ly To
wearines of religious dutys, and negligent performance of them at some
times. 3ly To Carnal lusts, by reason of the abundance of flatulent vapours
that annoy me And this maketh my very life a burden. so that I comfort my self with these hopes, either the Lord wil in pitty and compassion
provide for me so that I may live and not sin; or els he will shortly put an
end to this wretched life. And this I pray for. 4ly. To Melancholy scrupu-
losity, and a multitude of distractions that way. Lord thou seest how I am
oppressed, father undertake for me. It is the greif of my heart that I can
serv the no better. Oh! teach me, and enable me to do thy wil. oh! Lift
up the light of thy countenance for the Lords sake. Pardon my sins, heal
my backslidings mortify corruption, and heal in mercy my bodily infirmitys which both expose inevitably to sin, and make me with difficulty
attend my calling as thou Lord knowest. yet it is thy mercy that I have
a little time, and a little strength to serv thee, so good a master. oh that
I could do more! woe is me! I can do but little (of the little I do) for thee,
as my heart desireth.

I begin to think marriage wil be necessary for me (as an ordinance of
god appointed to maintain purity which my heart loveth) what ever the
event may be. Let me live no longer than I may live honestly good Lord.

I am ready to be desiring and hoping for a paradise in this world, Lord
pardon it. I earnestly desire Assurance of Gods Love, A heart to do all I do
from him and for him, weaned affections from the world and willingness
to dy. yesterday morning the Lord gaue a sweet meditation concerning
him.

Being in some expectation of my mothers coming to Harford on saturday: My thoughts and heart were too much running that way a great part
of the day.   yet in the evening the Lord let in somewhat of himself into my
heart, and let me tast an emptines in the creature yet some satisfaction in

himself. When I had done expecting her she came late in the evening.

My morning desires were on the sabbath that I might do nothing for my self to set forth my self, but all for god, and that I might mind god and not man in all the dutys thereoff.   the Lord pardon my falling short.

12 }
13 }

I find pride, and sensual outgoing of heart one while, and discouragement another while apt to prevail over me.   and fleshly lusts too are sometimes too strong for me. O wretched man that I am! which way so ever I turn me.   unfit to live becaus sinful at present and overborn, overpowered by corruptions so many.   unfit to dy because sensual and not savouring the things of another world: because myne iniquitys separate between me and my god and hide his face from me.   sorrows I meet with and temptations, and more I deserve than I feel, and therefore wel may I fear more.   oh I haue a carnal secure, proud, prophane, unbeleiving heart! that I wil complain off heavenly father, and not off thee. Thou art good, I am evil, thou art faithful I am unfaithful in the covenant.   oh I am ashamed that I dishonour my fathers hous so by feeding upon husks.   that I wrong and griev my head and husband so by not loving and delighting in his presence; by my liking other loves more than him ah Lord! I pul down evils upon others as wel as my self. Sicknesses, death of godly ones, wants, divisions have not my sins a hand in these miserys? oh Lord I am affraid of thy judgements upon my self and others. But spare thy people. I do beseech thee whatever become of me.

54 }
55 } March

On the last day in the Evening foregoing, a letter came to me from Mr Alcock, wherein he answered my scruples.   whereby I perceived that God had heard me in carrying my letters safely so far, and sending them from thence as they were directed toward Rowley. I bless god for one answer. I am in continuall expectation of another.

14

I found much weakness yet much gracious assistance and enlargement on the fast day. Lord let me find Acceptance and receiv answers of peace, both to my own wants, and the wants of others.

17

On that Last day I was much troubled with a multitude of thoughts about a journey to New Haven and Pequit. I strive and prayd against such diverting and disturbing distractions, yet they were too hard for me amidst my more serious studys. Lord pardon my wandrings, and pitty my weakness for thy mercy sake

18

Sabbath day morning / It grieveth me for my whoarish departures of heart from the Lord.   that I do not live upon him, to him, and walk with him in the world. And now methinks these sabbaths are blessed seasons wherein poor wandring harlots, may return to their husband again.   oh the boundles and unexhausted fountain of mercy that is with god and christ to entertain such again as I am! why behold! I come unto the thou art the Lord my God. My soul desireth communion with god, and Grace from him this day to enable me to serv him in sincerity so long as I live, (and not my self) and to fit me for everlasting fellowship with him in another world The Lord maketh me more than ordinary earnest in prayer that he would bless my ministry to the souls of his people this day. oh Lord! Rebuke pride, and selfishness that they marr not all I doe./ Though vain thoughts and pride and carnal lusts are rife and prevalent in me, and what I would do Lord I cannot, yet I bless thee that I haue time and heart to mourn for what I do amiss.

In the evening after the sabbath came news to me of Mr Winthrop's coming to New-Haven. On the 2d day God prosper'd my endeavours so, that I got 2 good horses at wethersfield and J. Latimore[38] to carry back my mother, which was performed with much eas to her upon the 3d day. I found Mr Winthrop staying longer there than some expected, not without thoughts of my coming thither which he had heard off by Goodman Warner.[39] I had much adoe to speak with him, yet at last I obtain'd it the night I came thither. I left the letter foreintended to be sent unto Pequit with him to consider off seriously, which he did, and gave his answer as far as he could in so short a time the next day at noon; which answer see in my book of Epistles after the coppy of the said letter. Now the Lord's name be magnify'd who hath prosper'd my way, and affoarded me his best advice with far less trouble than I was aware of. Blessed be the Lord that causeth my counsellers to agree in their counsel that I may see more clearly what is his mind in that weighty busines. Especially I bless him from my heart that he giveth me any hopes of comfort in the prosecution of that intendment which hath been so exercizing in the beginnings thereof. that I have heard of the lives of my friends at Rowley, (though no letter which I marvel at) the Lord be blessed also.

These are principles which the Lord hath been teaching me by his afflicting dispensations this Winter

1. To rejoyce in acting according to a Rule, whatever the event be, good or evil. mind my work which is all duty; and let god alone with events, which is his work

[38] John Latimer figures largely in the early records of Weathersfield. At the time of his death in 1662 he was one of its wealthiest inhabitants, possessor of two slaves.
[39] The records give no indication of any Warner in Weathersfield at this time, but this may have been Andrew Warner of Hartford, one of the first settlers there, who later participated in the founding of Hadley.

2: Not to rejoyce much in any creature; thou knowst not whither it shall comfort or Torment thee.

3: Not to be troubled with evil before it come, sufficient is the trouble of the day, when it is come

4: To be humbly thankful for life, and health, and liberty to serv god hitherto; though I should enjoy them no longer.

5: To fight against Melancholy and unbeleiving thoughts not by debating with them (for so they are too hard for me) but by sleighting them and not attending to them.

APRIL

Annus 1655
March 31

Much pride, A common heart (sitting loos from god, not savouring the service of god) carnal lusts stirring and prevalent, are the Plagues that discover themselves this week. I loath and abhor judge and condemn my self for these. I fear and tremble lest the Lord should depart away from me, as I deserv and then woe to me! when the Lord departs away, besides whom miserable comforters are all my comforts. But who is a god like thee? that pardons iniquity and passeth by &c   oh Pardon all the multitudinous evils thou seest in me in the multitude of thy mercys. Pardon my inordinate affections to this world or any thing therein. Pardon my unbeleif and unnecessary disquieting cares. Pardon my distemper'd passions. Pardon my want of due watchfulnes and care against these or any other evils for thy sons sake. Amen. I receiv'd letters from Rowley this week wherein I perceiv that my friends there be wel, and the heart of my cousen (after myne received) is toward me as before. Blessed be the good name of my god who hath so far heard prayer, as to carry my letters safe thither, to giue them so good acceptance, to return me an answer, whereby I perceiv it is my way to go down speedily into the Bay. And what further to attend for the present I see not, but I hope the Lord wil direct when I come there. The Lord in mercy make me desirous as formerly to attend onely my duty and leav the rest to him. Lord increas my faith, and patience. /

I got Mr Newton[40] to pray with me on thursday night after a relation of the present difficultys which surround me wherewith he was much affected. Lord hear in heaven and give answers of peace.

April/
4.

At the lecture out of Job. 14. 2. Many cordials being propounded to strengthen the hearts of gods people Against bodily infirmitys and death it self: Me thoughts I felt an unspeakable unwortynes of any intrest in god

[40] Roger Newton was minister at Farmington, Connecticut.

and his grace at such times of need, because of the unspeakable vilenes of my heart which I feel, o that I could feel it more. Ah pride! frothines I haue not matter for good discours, nor a heart unto it. it grieveth me to think of my folly and madnes. ah! I do serv my self and not my god in all I doe.

APRIL FROM THE 8 TO

On the sabbath day morning, (having prepared to preach the 2 dayes before and fully intending it) I awaked with a very sore throat, so that I perceived my mouth was stop't for that day. Mr stow[41] being in the town by a providence supply'd the place. It was a sacrament day and I ventured out (hooded) before noon, but afternoon *again* durst not. I kept hous all that week, being much pained in swallowing my spittle, and so over-flowed with rhewm that If I forbare spitting my throat grew painful with drines. This ilnes marrd my stomack utterly, (especially by the nauseous tast of the fleum at the beginning and latter end thereoff) mightily en-feebled my spirits, wasted my moysture and made me feaverish. I used principally burnt wine, which almost set me in a swoon divers times, yet I think did me good. At the latter end of the week growing something better I ventured out to wethersfield-hooded. whence I had a hors brought me according to agreement on munday and on Tuesday I set forth for the Bay. The motives that hasten'd me were these. 1. I found my ilnes con-tinue and no means there to help me. 2ly I conceived journeying might do me good as much as physick, if I could keep from could. 3. To redeem the spring time for marrying or taking physick, or both. God brought me thorow comfortably in 2 dayes from springfield to Roxbury, much bet-tered (though wearied) with my journey. staying a day in the Bay and consulting with Mr Alcock (who advized to proceed with the busines of marriage In the 1st place) I reach't Rowley on the saturday. / On mun-day ensueing I dined and discoursed with Mr Rogers about the great busines. He could by noe means concur with the other physicians in ad-vizing first to marriage and afterward to taking physick, for many rea-sons by him alledged; but thought it meet 1. to rectify the habit of my body and afterward to proceed. I was distressed at the hearing of his opin-ion, because it stil made the case more difficult. I prayd to the god of heav-en and such was his mercy to me, that after a little reasoning about the case, and fuller declaration of my ilness &c. Mr Rogers his mind was quite altered, and he declared himself free and ready to further the consum-

April 17

---

[41] Samuel Stow, of Middletown, Connecticut, graduated from Harvard in 1645, served as minister for a time at Middletown and later at Simsbury but was never permanently settled at any church.

mation thereof with all possible speed. And so he contrived the busines and wrought it with them whom it concerned, that it was then publish't, and I was to return again and be contracted the next friday sev'night. and so I left my friends with determination so to return. Yet after I was gone from thence. My own weakness (which formerly perplexed me at such times) setting in with Mr Rogers his scruples did much trouble me, and caus me to questeon, whither it were my way to marry, before the use of more means, and to run such a hazzard as that of my life and health without an apparent necessity, before I had tryed the utmost that physick could doe. I repaired to Mr Alcock with all speed again to speak with him and object unto him for my farther satisfaction.

1: He told me that he hoped my diseas might be cured by physick; but It would be a long and teadious and far more difficult cure, then he hoped it would be by marriage, and astringent cordials afterward. And he had no heart to go the farther way about when as he might haue a nearer way by providence offer'd him.

2: He told me divers experiences of the success of this cours in like distempers. An example of one just affected like my self before his marriage, who was grievously perplexed with it, yet went on with it and did very wel after, and hath divers children living at this day. And so of divers others who have taken this cours with good success.

3: He told me that mine was not vera Gon:[42] as he could prove nor the excretio *(which happened by the presence of such a friend)* seminis but quasi sudor partium genitatium: as a little alumn wil caus the mouth to fil with water, so a little acrimony gathering there, causeth humours to flow thither amain, which might come away in great quantity, and yet there be plenty of veri seminis behind. And so I found it to be.

4ly. He told me that which made me so fearful, made him fearles, and gave him the more hopes, that marriage would take away the caus of that distemper, which was naturalis impulsus seu instinctus irresistibilis.

These things together with the consideration. 1. of my unsettled condition wherein I cannot attend rules of Physick with any conveniency. 2ly off the great charge and expences I must be at for a continued cours of Physick and diet better than ordinary. 3ly of my inability with comfort and

---

[42] The word intended here is obviously gonorrhea; but I have thought it best not to expand the abbreviation, because former accounts of Wigglesworth's life have professed to be mystified with regard to the disease of which Wigglesworth so frequently complains. It seems indisputable from the symptoms described and from this direct statement that Wigglesworth thought that he had gonorrhea. Whether his disease was actually gonorrhea, of course, no one can say.

honesty to live long as I am single. 4ly off the little hopes to prevayl against rebellious nature, which is disquieted rather than overcome by physick in statu presenti. These things make it pretty clear to me that god calleth to a speedy change of my condition, which I therefore desire to attend as a duty that god calleth unto, leaving my life and health in his hands. And oh! that I had a meek spirit to submit to his good pleasure. A beleiving heart! and a judicious mind to see clearly that this is my way at all times

I went up at the time appointed and was contracted on friday (May   ) God made this journey more comfortable to me, refreshing me and cheering me among my dearest friends. yet with the admixture of the same affliction as formerly, though something moderated blessed be God! I was troubled to think that they were not willing to have the wedding before the election, and so to drive a month at least it may be two months because the magistrates would all be absent at that time. yet here again providence appeared sweetly in bowing their spirits to issue it within a fourt-night, and so before the Election; And all things we found conspiring to further our intendment, Taylors ready to do the work in time, merchants ready to take provisions for shopp commoditys, &c. blessed be god! who worketh all our works in us and for us. oh! I am ashamed of my frothines   may 18. and vanity and fruitless conversation, and sensuality and all those sins whereby I am offending so good a god. saturday./ May

I was somewhat perplexed also at my return into the bay after my contraction, concerning the lawfulness of marrying with a Kinswoman, because the mothers sister is forbidden; now sister in scripture language is put for a Kinswoman sometimes. I spent some time about it and the Lord gaue me comfortable satisfaction in this point also, that my scruple was Invalid.

At the time appointed with fear and trembling I came to Rowley to be   which was married. The great arguments unto me were, 1: Physicians counsel: 2ly   on friday the institution of marryage by god himself for the preservation of purity   may 18. and chastity, which with most humble and hearty prayers I have begged and stil wil beg of the Lord. so that I went about the business which god call'd me to attend And consummated it now is by the will of god May 18. 1655./ oh Lord! let my cry come up unto thee for all the blessings of a marryed estate, A heart sutable thereto, chastity especially thereby, and life and health if it be thy will. oh crown thy own ordinance with thy blessing, that it may appear it is not in vain to wait upon thee in the wayes of thy own appointment   *I feel the stirrings and strongly of my former distemper even after the use of marriage the next day which makes me exceeding afraid. I know not how to keep company with my dearest friend but it is with me as formerly in some days already.* oh pitty the poorest and vilest of thy creatures for the Lords sake, And let not thy servants be a curs each to other but a blessing in this new relation

I have been 3 times at the Bay since my wedding. the first time I met my father in Law from England the very next week after the marriage. blessed be god! The 2d time I got a sore cold by preaching at Mauldon. The 3d time I got a surfet, fell into a loosnes yet (through mercy) made a shift to get well home, where I was much weakned. My strength is wel recover'd again now I thank god this present. 10 of July. But these ilnesses, colds rhewms and keeping the hous so much have made me so tender that I cannot preach but catch a grievous cold. yea these continued colds disable me to any service either in family or in publick. And through a light and frothy heart I cannot honour god with the little remaynder of strength which I have this (God knowes) is my daly grief, that I can do so little for god. that I am unfaithful in the talent I haue and so unworthy to be trusted with more strength.

This disabling me from service is some matter of exercise to my faith and patience. Hereby The Lord hath made me more to think off my unworthyness to be honourd with the service of god. And more to prize and long after ability to serv god. And more thankful that he hath put me upon publick service now so oft these 8 sermons since I came from Harford. my soul blesseth the Lord when he giveth me any opportunity and ability to serv him in that way. And this is some quieting to me that the Lord hath dealt better than my fears with me already; in that I have been confined so long to home, and yet so little molested with my ordinary distemper. oh Let god be magnify'd! Besides I consider affliction is gods furnace, it shall purge away filth; so that I shall be fitter either to live better, or dy happier, having a weightier crown of glory. oh Lord! increas my faith and patience

About the 17th of July I went to the Bay carrying my wife with me. where much of god appear'd both in our comfortable going and return, (though I much fear'd the prevailing of rhewm to my great affliction, yet the Lord prevented it) and also much of god in expediting my occasions; which were with the Physician, about a parcel of corn disposing of (which providence had taken good order for in my absence) and about Maldon Invitation; Blessed be god for all his benefits. But oh my ill requitalls of the Lords love! Much frothyness pride, *carnal lusts also exceeding* prevailing *Lord forgive my intemperance in the use of marriage for thy sons sake.*

July 28   I am infinitely indebted unto the Lord that gives me so much comfort

in a married estate contrary to my fears; for this I wil prais him whilest I
haue a being

I am now about the use of means against my rhewm which I find very
prevalent still. therefore the Lord shew's me what need to beg his blessing without which means avayl not; therefore I desire others to beg it for
me, to the end I might be set at liberty to serv god and his people.

My earnest prayer this sabbath is that I may be fitted (by spiritual blessings receiv'd from god in the way of his ordinances) for life or death, both
which I find my self very unfit for. for I fear death, and I haue done
(woe is me!) little for god; and yet to live without more grace ah! to
how little purpose is?

I have been this morning studying for what caus the Lord may contend
with me in this my weakness, which stil troubles me much, Rhewm I
mean. yet cannot conclude what it is; I am guilty of many evils and much
unprofit. Nonimprovement of the talent I haue at present makes me unworthy of more strength; and so much selfishness in all I do, might justly
provoke the Lord to disable me from doing any thing. but the Lord is my
witness these things are my burden. Lord do not plague me for that which
above all things I desire and pray to be rid off! And now with god and for
god I do begin to study this day, whose glory and Kingdom I desire by all
means to promote, the good Lord enable me to honour him, for that I account my greatest happiness in this world.

I went into the Bay August the 4th and preacht at Maldon twice on the
sabbath. Before my preching there (and so before my preaching at Rowley
the next sabbath) I had such serious meditations as these: The voyce of
the Lords rod unto me at the present is this; Know thou that thou art utterly unworthy to serv me. whereto my heart answereth: True Lord
I own my vilenes, my pride, my sensuality my frothynes, my filthynes &c.
these make me unworthy to make mention of the Lords name. It is thy un-
deserved free mercy (for which I thank thee) that thou hast given me opportunity and strength to serv the so long, and that I may stil do it once
more. And for the future, if the Lord say he hath no pleasure in me, Loe!
here am I, desiring to lay my mouth in the dust in humble submission to
him: the Lord is righteous if he deal thus with me; yea he is merciful and
gracious that he hath dealt so no sooner. Lord why do I survive, when
those that were so much better are taken away? some off them in their
beginnings; as Mr Theophilus Eaton[43] of New Haven lately chosen a

[43] Theophilus Eaton, one of the original patentees of the Massachusetts Bay Company, was the founder with John Davenport of the New Haven Colony. He was
governor of the colony, re-elected annually, until his death.

magistrate, with his godly wife, both deceased within a few dayes time.

☞ when I was at Maldon; I told them that I thought it would be a tempting of Providence to accept of their Invitation, for

1. I found preaching very hazzardful at present in that it exposed to such dangerous coulds

2. It was feared that my strength would never sute with double work[44] After the debating this matter too and fro they left me to consider more of it a while. Here, upon further consideration; I could not satisfy my self in the force of my former argument: becaus the harm I found by preaching was principally (if not onely) in the time of the general visitation by colds;

August since, all that I haue found hath been onely some little return of a sore throat, that hath soon gone away again. yea I found no great harm by my sabbath dayes work at Maldon, though the wether were very cold and wet.   And for the 2d Argument. double work in so small a congregation is not much more then single work in a great one; and if it be more, yet there are other things to ballance it. these things considered made me promis to deliberate more about it for another fourt'-night; I asked Mr Alcocks advice, who told me he thought neither of these plea's of such weight as to ground a refusal of this Invitation upon them. He thought I might hope to be better in a settled way; and hoped wel It would be better with me hereafter; And to help the double work, I might preach the less while. off the same mind was my Uncle Reyner.[45]

15   When I preach't at Rowley August the 12. I found my self very faint ☞ and feeble all the forenoon and just until I began, yet through mercy assisted with more then ordinary strength in the work (when I am weak then am I strong) And I find (through Gods mercy) no great harm afterwards onely weaknes by much sweat. Mr Philips[46] in the forenoon preacht upon this point: The people of God take notice of mercy in the sorest afflictions. I assent to this trueth. I can (I thank God) take notice of much mercy though sore afflicted. 1. Its mercy I had so long a time of peace. 2ly Moderation of the affliction. 3ly support from god under affliction. 4. sanctify'd use of affliction, my heart train'd up under it to humility, faith patience, and heavenly affections. 5. seasonable redemption from afflictions at my earnest prayers. the Lord be magnifyd.

August 1655 I have been meditating what caus I have to be thankful, and to shew it in

[44] Large congregations usually had two ministers, one called pastor and the other teacher. When one man served both functions, he did "double work."

[45] Probably the Reverend John Reyner.

[46] Samuel Phillips, son of the Reverend George Phillips of Watertown, graduated from Harvard in 1650 and in 1651 joined Ezekiel Rogers as minister of Rowley.

a fruitful conversation to the glory of god. my soul desireth to be so; Lord help me herein. And as I follow'd God by fayth in the matter of marriage beyond sence, and have found a blessing: so I desire to do in this Invitation to Mauldon, if the Lord appear therein, and to beleiv (yea I do beleiv) that if he call he will enable thereto.

oh my god! it grieveth me to think of my vain and fruitless conversation, that I can do so little for thee, so much against thee. It grieveth me that in the fiery furnace my dross should stil remain; my pride, frothines, sensuality, filthines. Ah Lord deliver me from these this day, and evermore. oh giue me more grace and strength to serv thee though I deserv it not. for thou seest how my spiritual plagues, and bodily weaknesses, prevail over me. *August 15 16.*

At my next being in the Bay I found less incouragement to yield unto Maldons invitation than before. For having taken it into consideration a fourt'night longer and finding my self rather wors, it seemed a barr put in by providence to stop further proceedings. so according to advice of friends I wholy putt by the motion upon the onely ground of present unfitness for any constant service. the wil of the Lord be done; how cross soever unto mine. Since I beg earnestly his blessing upon the cours of physick I am about, knowing that if he say the word they shal do me good, not els. To this end I haue beggd the prayers of divers this being a season of fayth and prayer. I find some assaults of temptation to distrust in respect of outward sustenance in case of disability to service. but by the grace of god I do in some measure trust in his fatherly providence who wil not leav me nor forsake me: who wil giue grace and glory &c. *August September*

I receiv'd the Lords supper here on the sabbath. Before and att which the Lord came in sweetly to discover and affect my heart with sin, making me sensible of my need of whole christ; prophet priest and King, making all of christ precious and desirable; and so perswading me of the gift of his son to be bread of life to me. My longing desire is to walk worthy of him, to be fruitful in my conversation, and I mourn for my falling short hereoff. *September 2d*

The next sabbath I preach here with more than ordinary assistance *10*

It is a time of more than ordinary trouble because I am yet unsettled winter approaching, and know not what to doe about it becaus my weaknes and colds stil continue and I fear in cold wether it should be wors with me. the matter of my trouble are such things as these.

1 My present weaknes unfitting me for almost any service or, making it very difficult	Be thankful that thy weaknes is not sicknes. Heretofore thou hast sought others good neglecting thy own;

but now thou art hindred from doing that thou might take time to be getting and growing.

2ly Fear of increas of weaknes as the cold increaseth because it is an extraordinary propensity to take cold at my nosthrils.

3ly Difficulty in concluding about my winter aboad: If I undertake any publick work I fear lest I should fail their expectations. If I sit stil winter wil come on and I must do nothing, which is very cross to my desires of being serviceable to God.

I will lead the blind in a way they have not known.

Call upon me in the day of trouble, and I wil hear thee and thou shalt glorify me.

Faithful is he that hath promised and wil do it

He hath done it heretofore.

Christ himself my Lord had not a hole to put his head in.

4ly My mother and sister are come to me from New Haven, and I haue no hous to put my own head in much less room for them. which is discourageing unto them whom I have brought from a settled to an unsettled estate.

5ly. If we all liue in an unsettled way, it wil soon spend all we haue and bring us to penury, yet so it must be if I be disabled from service

Blessed be God that we haue friends willing to entertain us thus long.

Be thankful for what is already layd in against a time of need. For the future, my heavenly father wil provide, by means (perhaps) that we know not.

6ly Where we are, if he [torn] should continue it wil be uncomfortable to winter for cold *and especially to me seeing we can't lay severally without obloquy and reproach neither can we lay together without exposing me to the return of grievous disease.*

God will guide and provide.

He hath done so in troubles as great as these and therefore he can do it and will do it

In Memoriall of his former mercys received in answer to prayer and off all his goodnes hitherto I wil erect

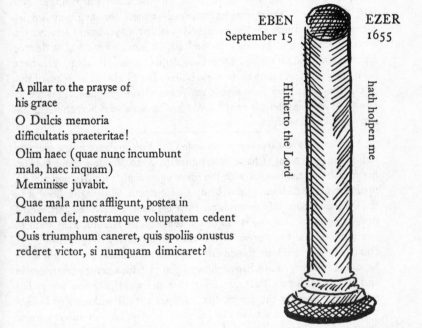

EBEN   EZER
September 15   1655

A pillar to the prayse of
his grace
O Dulcis memoria
difficultatis praeteritae!

Olim haec (quae nunc incumbunt
mala, haec inquam)
Meminisse juvabit.

Quae mala nunc affligunt, postea in
Laudem dei, nostramque voluptatem cedent

Quis triumphum caneret, quis spoliis onustus
rederet victor, si numquam dimicaret?

Hitherto the Lord   hath holpen me

some night pollution escaped me notwithstanding my earnest prayer to the contrary which brought to mind my old sins now too much forgotten (as near as I remember the thoughts that then I had) together with my later sins unto seeming one that had received so many mercies from the Lord   O unthankfulness unthankfulness when shall I get rid of thee.

sabbath.
september

The same week I went to the Bay; About my mothers goods left at Boston, which disposed off the best I could. About further directions from the physician; About Maldon busines with some further inclinations to it upon the grounds above specify'd where I found them that I spake withall still earnest in their desires after me and that they needed not that I should beginn it afresh. I defer'd any conclusion till Mr Hill[47] come up to Ipswich to the generall training. the good Lord guid me in a right way. amen.

I haue been musing about this point, that God is. besides what arguments I read in others these are presented to me. 1. If there were no god mens hearts would not be full of enmity against god as they are. ergo there is a God. 2. Once I was blind, but now I see, once dead but now alive, once loving sin and hating holines; who made this change? Not self; for to me beleiving was impossible. Not men, for then why are not others converted that are less hardened in sin, or why was not I converted sooner (whilest it was easier) nor Sathan; he is not such a fool to destroy his own kingdom; therefore it was God, ergo God is. 3ly My prayers have been answer'd from time to time, ergo there Is a God who hath heard me. If there were no God, how should my prayers haue been heard. whoever doubts of his being let me never doubt it who haue seen him and felt him not onely heard off him.

October
7th

October
55

After many and earnest prayers unto God For guidance in the weighty busines of settlement, I haue determined to go to Maldon about a 14:n. hence. I issued the busines with the messengers sent from Maldon church upon the generall training day being October 4th. I hope the Lord is in this determination My grounds are such as these. 1: God requireth and I desire to do service as my strength wil bear; and I feel not such want of strength but that I can preach without prejudice to my body; Although I fear it, that my weaknes should encreas with the winter, yet the physician hopes the contrary, and I haue followed god by faith against greater feares and prospered therein heretofore. To what end was the former mercy but to train me to it for the future. 2ly The place is stil without supply notwithstanding their endeavours to get a supply. 3ly They continue earnest in their desires. renewing their former sute. If they be willing to adventure upon my weaknes, why should not I adventure upon the work. 4ly I found some beginnings of amendment by the abatement of rhewm and hopes of good. by the use of oil against my aptness to get cold. God had in part removed the onely impediment; and why should I stand out any longer. 5ly we cannot winter here. Because the hous is too cold, becaus the room too strait (here is not a private room for me) because also *we must lay together constantly which I can't bare*. And to remove, as good to Maldon for

[47] Joseph Hills was the first representative of the town of Malden in the General Court of Massachusetts and later was speaker of the House of Deputies. He created a scandal in the colony by following the earlier example of Governor Bellingham in presiding at his own wedding (see below, p. 99). He had also been one of the supporters of Marmaduke Mathews, the previous minister of Malden, who had been chosen without approval of the General Court and who was consequently ousted.

ought I know as any where; And in respect of charges I hope better: thus divine providence seemeth not onely to invite but to necessitate hereunto./ And what the Lord calleth unto he will fit for   Lord increas my faith.

Myne inordinate affection unto creatures and too must [*sic*] trusting to the bountiful provision that god hath made for us, is a grief to my heart because a dishonour and grief to the Lord

Octo-
ber

I find my corruptions very strong. As pride Inordinate affection to creatures, frothines, empty and fruitles conversation, undutifulnes to my mother, deadheartednes and wandrings in gods worship; these are my great burden, which I come to the Lord to rid me off upon this day of spiritual blessings. I desire The sincere milk of the word that I may grow thereby in grace.

7

(wednesday) [three words in shorthand undecipherable] aggredior opus hodiernum, desiring much to do all that I do for god. ah Lord giue me more grace to honour thee in thought word and deed; it is my grief I do it so little.

10.

Friday. Cum Deo To whose glory be this written. When I feel my own present weakness to be such, I am apt to be affraid lest I should be un-serviceable at Maldon by the coldness of winter, and live upon expences unprofitably. Yet I desire not to giue way to discouragement; For 1: I am in Gods way to remove thither and cast myself upon Gods providence to see what he will do for me and by me. Not onely gods voyce in them (whose desire is so constant and necessity so great) call's me to it, but he hath all along inclined my spirit unto it, and now his providence driveth me to it as it were perforce, and hath incouraged to it by beginnings of amend-ment (although it sticketh in the birth). Now all that I haue to mind is duty vizt to obey Gods voyce let the event be what he will. 2ly He is able to prevent my feares and strengthen me above my hopes; as my former experience can witness. 3ly He hath promised to be with me in his way and to order all occurrences for glory to himself; good to me and to his peo-ple. And what would I more. Lord strengthen my fayth to beleev and follow thee in this busines; and to wayt thy good pleasure; yea to submit to thy will, that If thou say I haue no pleasure in the my heart may say Let the Lord do with me what seemeth him good. If it be thy will Lord send health and strength that I may glorify thy name and do good to thy poor people. If not oh Lord teach me to ly at thy foot. So haue I prayd this day, and so will I pray, till the Lord look down from heaven.

12

October

oh 'tis good for me to draw near to god! The Lord hath met with me this day according to my wish.   he hath spoken to my heart, he hath melted it into teares by his truth. I haue heard even such things as I would this day,

october 55
sabbath 14

how all the saints are such as haue purify'd themselues, and ought to do it more and more. Why purity is that I want Lord, which I mourn after, 'tis that I would. oh giue me what thou requirest, and then require what thou wilt. Giue more earnest and constant desires and effectuall endeavours after it. I am affraid lest I desire health more then holyness (though I desire that also that I might haue opportunity for further exercise of holines) but what good wil my life or health do me good Lord If I liue not to thy prais and honour? oh pitty me, and grant encreas of both if it be thy will. And make this truth a means of it and this day a beginning of it.

october 55   [Blank page]

February 20 toward night being wednesday my wife began to travail, and had sore paines   The nearnes of my bed to hers made me hear all the nois. her pangs pained my heart, broke my sleep the most off that night, I lay sighing, sweating, praying, almost fainting through wearines before morning. The next day. the spleen much enfeebled me, and setting in with grief took away my strength, my heart was smitten within me, and as sleep departed from myne eyes so my stomack abhorred meat. I was brought very low and knew not how to pass away another night; For so long as my love lay crying I lay sweating, and groaning. I was now apt to be hasty and impatient, but the Lord made me desirous to stoop to his wil (if he should take away her whom he had given, much more) if he should onely prolong her pains (himself supporting) and in time restore her. Being brought to this the Lord gaue some support to my heart   After about midnight he sent me the glad tidings of a daughter that and the mother both living; after she had been in paines about 30 houres or more.   oh Let the Lord be magnifyd who heareth the poor chatterings of his prisoners; who wil lay no more than he enableth to bear. 2 Lessons the Lord hath taught me by this. 1 If the evil of sorrow be so great how evil then in [is?] sin the caus off it

2: If the dolours of child-bearing be so bitter (which may be onely a fatherly chastizement) then how dreadful are the pangs of eternal death

After our child was about a Fourtnight old it was much afflicted with a sore mouth, which continued near 3 weeks, accompanyd with griping and loosnes and sore hips./

shee had in this time 2 pittiful nights, especially the one of them. At that time 2 things I desir'd of the Lord 1. A heart to subject my wisdom and wil to his touching the childs life or Extremity. he knows what is best, and is as tenderly affected as I, and much more. 2. That I may maintain good thoughts of god while he afflicts   amare deum castigantem   I haue giuen up my daughter to him with all my heart desiring she may be his, rejoycing he hath giuen me a child to giue up to him. And shall he not do with his own as he will, either to afflict it or take it to himself. His glory is better than the eas of the creature, and yet his glory shall be coincident with our good.

After this the Lord mercifully recovered it, and it is now grown and come to be a quarter old. Friday May 16.   1656

1656

[Two blank pages]

Fons vitae me vivifica. pudet me penitus sensualitatis et mutilitatis meae domine. quo usque differs preces meas exaudire? tu es vita mea, fac ut ego vivam per te. ne sim carnalis adhuc dum verbum spiritualis vitae praedico. Aperi os meum ut labia mea celebrent te, non modo sabbato sed quotidie. vivant alii per verbum tuum ut fructus aliquos videam. et jam cum deo et christo opus aggredior huius sabbati. tu mihi princip. tu mihi finis eris. Dec. 14. idem a merid.

Attolle lumen vultus tui super me domine Corruant superbia, sensualitas, iracundia, vanitas cogitationum et verborum hodie medullitus et ex animo precor./ Lubens gaudensque tibi hodie servio in Evangelio filii tui, ovitulare mihi. sabbat D. 21.

December 27. I haue been greatly exercised with the spleen these sundry weeks, and yet I find no abatement of it. I know not what god wil do with me. I desire to follow him by faith, when I cannot by sence. Blessed be his name that yet I haue a little strength to serv him. I desire to serv my god this day if I know what my heart desires; Lord strengthen me.

sabbath December 28. Lord I am going to hear what thou wilt speak to me or by me, I am to preach out of *Psalms* 119 49 concerning living by faith; oh teach me this blessed lesson! and others by me. Tu mihi princip. tu mihi finis.

Tibi domine Jesu, tuus sum, et tibi studeo. January 1 thursday.

Cum deo et christo. princip. et fine. January 2.

ah Lord spiritualize my mind and heart to be conversant about the doctrine of the saints future glory. tuo nomine, et robore et propter te hodie domine saturday January 3.

Sabbath January 4. Lord fit me for thy heavenly truth (concerning the saints future glory) sanctify me by it assure me of mine interest in it, that the thoughts of death may not dismay me.

[Half line undecipherable]

Saturday. Sis mihi principium, sis mihi finis &c. dolet me ob carnales affectiones et passiones iracundas domine.

11

Sabbath. Lord I am not worthy to be owned or pittied by the, a sink of sin! so frowardly passionate, so earthly and carnal as I have bin this week past. for the Lords sake hide not away thy face this day. oh! when wilt thou come to me? when wilt thou mortify these lusts, when wilt thou giue me a heart to savour the things of god above all other things? oh that it might be this day! I wil beg, I wil wait for the Lord's salvation. and now with gods assistance for god this day.

Ah Lord! my soul longs yea it even faints for thy salvation: I haue desired and long begged power against the carnality of my heart, that this lust might dy, and the contrary grace be increased: but yet I find my heart as carnal as some years since for ought I can tell. the world I can savour the things of god I cannot. Lord! why witholdest thou thy spirit which thou hast promised to them that ask it? thou hast kept me waiting, but given me no sensible answer these many years. Wil thy own glory, wil christs merits, will thy promis wherein thou hast made me hope prevail any thing with the? why, good Lord then at last be found of me, this day. sabbath. January 25.

29

A deo et ad deum thursday. January 29.

idem. thursday. *Lord without thee I can do nothing   Leave me not to my own understanding*.

4 things I earnestly beg this day. the light of thy Countenance oh Lord, the efficacy of thy grace to subdue my lusts and make me more fruitful, the assistance of thy spirit in the work of the ministry that I may do it with an enlarged heart and utterance and for thee, Finally the salvation, and Edification of this poor people. Fiat domine, fiat idem ex corde precor February 8. sabbath. mortify Lord these earthly members which stake me down to the things of this world. &c.

saturday. February 14. Lord make me to understand thy word aright oh leav me not to my own mistakes. make me to delight more abundantly in thy self and service for the Lords sake, and fit me for thy day. amen

oh my god I bless the for any mesure of advantage against my sinful neglect of good discours. Lord increas thy grace in me and mortify corruption more and more. oh thou that hearest prayer, answer gratiously my long and longing desires after the Light of that countenance, and Heavenly mindedness this day. [Two words undecipherable]   sabbath. february 15.

[Two words undecipherable] *Lord let curiousness die this day for the Lord sake   I feel and I fear it.*

Oh Lord I do in some measure hunger after good by thy word this day which sutes my heart   plague out of Mathew 6. 28. 29. 30. and Collossians 3. 5. Coveting which is idolatry. It grieveth me to find so much idolatry in my self after all means to the contrary.   march 29.

In April I went to Rowley (the week after the elders went up to Harford) and tarry'd a Fourtnight, being sorely exercised with a cold most of that while.   blessed be the Lord we got safe home.

1657

This day is appointed for an issue about my settlement. Lord I look up to thee for wisdom and guidance in so sollemn a busines. I haue all along been exercised with discouragements since I came hither. 1. with mr Hills marrying of himself which I understood to be very ridiculous in the opinion of the courtry where it was noised. 2. with the contestations between the Town and the Treasurer about the hous I live in. 3 with the peoples slownes in keeping their seasons of bringing in, and making good their engagements. 4. with the returns of my nightly distemper occasioned by study about church Goverment, and my want of insight thereinto, or of strength to attain it: 5. with fears of Mr Hills judgement about baptism; he being an elder elect. now finding him staggering or unsound I held it altogether unsafe to let his ordination proceed. so I used means to bring out his opinion and prevent the other. The Lord hath in some measure removed all these, qua discouragements, so far as I find my self inclinable to the place and people and work of christ among them. There is yet another afflicting thing; And that is a multitude of great black buggs which do swarm all over the hous no room nor place free, no cupboard, pot, &c. like Pharaohs froggs. And they eat all kind of food and we apprehend they haue eaten some cloaths also. I am loath to make this a discouragement (though a great affliction) because I hope it may be removed in some measure by plaistering the chimneys and stopping their holes, or els by building new chimneys of brick. or if there be no remedy by building a hous in another place.

May. 19.
tuesday
1657

There seem's to be a clear call of god unto office-work. For. 1. Here is a poor desolate people alwayes without an officer til they got a bad one and were glad to be rid of him. but now brought lower then ever. 2. This people unanimous, importunate, constant in desiring me. 3 The neighbours also resorting much unto us. 4 Gods marvelous work in carrying me (so weak) through the difficulty of the work in this place. his presence with me here hath been such as this seems to be the place. 5. I apprehend this place both in respect of nearness to the bay and many other ways most sutable to my weaknes. 6 The constant inclination of my own spirit unto it notwithstanding all discouragements, and not to any other; though I haue not been without some sollicitations.

[Here the diary proper ends. The remainder of the book contains miscellaneous notes and reflections, written mainly in shorthand and beginning at the other end of the volume.]

[Beginning at the other end of the volume]

I am afraid of drawing near God in so holy an ordinance for I cant find any power to prize Christ and communion with him at some times   Oh if God leave me to the pretending of my own heart as I deserve he should I shall no more value him than the dry dust I tread under my feet and I shall find my heart so many times left when I will come nearest God   For this cause I am afraid

My unbelieving heart saith I have backslidden so oft so daily continued and laid under the power of my backslidings so long and so few comings out of them and will the Lord accept of me   Shall I be welcome if I return   Will his heart be toward me?

[Three-quarters of a page blank]

I had occasion about the ijth of February to go and visit Jeremy Peck[48] *and took occasion to speak what a blessed thing it was to seek and serve the Lord to have him for our portion who only was an abiding friend. So I fell into discourse with him about his soul. He told me he still saw himself sinful and miserable and though he had precious means yet he could not be sensible of it   He found he could do nothing notwithstanding all his purposes and resolutions   I told him true yet God will do nothing without ourselves. There is the more need to cry restlessly for help. Among other things I advised him to be plain in confession of sin particularly before God.* He answer'd me that he was affraid to confess his sins before god, because he had heard Mr Davenport say, take heed when thou comest before god to confess sin that god enter not into judgment with thee, and condemn the out of thyne owne mouth. I told him that was when we confess but are not desirous to forsake.

[Two-thirds of a page blank]

A man was afraid he had sinned against the Holy Ghost and came to a minister who answered him in short hast thou sinned that sin   Why comest thou to me those that have committed that sin are not wont to be sorry for it. This being told her by her mother gave her some comfort at present but continued not after she had resort to that first Isaiah 16. Though your sins be as crimson yet they shall be

---

[48] Jeremiah Peck, a student at Harvard from 1653 to 1656, was schoolmaster at Guilford, Connecticut, from 1656 to 1660 and later a minister.

as wool. After God directed me to that book called The Christian's Daily Walk of Mister Scudder[49] Spoke to the comfort of such as are so buried with temptation in it there was a description of the sin against the Holy Ghost He showed that these temptations so blasphemous they were the devil's sins and the soul's burden wherein I had great comfort by God's mercy yet not free from temptation. I was at a conference where there was a question how to discern the temptation of Satan from those of our own concupiscence in which I reaped much resolution and comfort. In this condition the Lord brought me to see all my duties which I had rested in were nothing worth The Lord brought me to resolve with myself though he kill me yet will I trust in him If I must [be] damned yet it shall be in the way of obedience as far as God enabled me. And I was in some measure contented though I should be damned. But the Lord left me not long in this hopeless estate but directed Mister Newman[50] to preach out of Isaiah 66.2. To him that is poor and of contrite spirit will I look He showed what the soul must be to whom the lord will look and how the Lord worked this poverty of spirit. And the qualifications of a soul truly poor in spirit so that by God's mercy I had abundance of unspeakable comfort in the time of his preaching this sermon He preached out of Revelation 2. 4 5 thou hast left thy first love He said this was the first love in conversion and that every true convert had this first love and that was Jesus Christ and showed how this love was Christian indeed to every spiritual object to God and his word ordinances people &c. And how the soul did admire Jesus Christ and free grace that he was to it the chief of 10000 In this time I had very much spiritual joy I heard Mister Flint[51] out of Isaiah 57. 16. He showed God contends with every soul before he speaks peace to it whereby I was encouraged that the Lord had spoken peace to me

I doubted how I loved Christ

It was answered our love to Christ did appear in our love to his word ordinances people as we saw Christ in them

[One page blank]

November 26. 1654 At a private meeting

Rules of daly practise for living to God.

1: Know and consider what is thy duty

2ly. Look up to christ as thy head for strength

3ly Be deeply sensible of thy unworthynes of any help from him

4ly Be thankful for what he gives

[49] Henry Scudder, *The Christians Daily Walke in Holy Securitie and Peace* (London, 1627).

[50] Samuel Newman, educated at Oxford, came to New England in the 1630's and eventually became minister at Rehoboth.

[51] Henry Flint came to New England in 1635 and became minister at Braintree.

5ly Improve it, and be doing with what he giveth wayting with patience for more assistance.

In meditation

---

objection: What if god deny me the spiritual grace which I want?   I seek him but find little coming.

Answer

1 By this means God wil make thee deeply sensible to thy own vilenes and of the vastnes of thy wants.

2: Hereby He wil make thee more earnest in desires after grace to do better

3ly He wil accept thy wil for thy deed

4ly. He wil by degrees increas spiritual strength in what manner, measure and season he seeth fit

so that it is not in vain to continue praying though thou feel little good come in for the present.

[One page blank]

Considerations against Pride

Consider. 'Tis a sin committed with greatest ingratitude. For 'tis not onely against the god that made, the tender father who has nourish't the, kept thee fed the, (not with bread and water of affliction, but bountifull allowance) whose everlasting armes have supported thee, who brought the over the deeps out of a place of sin and sorrow's into a good land flowing with milk and hony, abounding with heavenly manna, who hath preserv'd the in so many fearful dangers, from the fury of so many raging devils: who when he hath had the at advantage nevertheles hath pitty'd the and spared the with astonishing long sufferance; who hath striven with thee by his spirit though griev'd many a time, though quench't with thy filthy lusts: who hath taken the from servile imployment to attend upon him in a better way, though against thy will: who hath pluck't the out of sathans jaws and the belly of hell at last, when he finally leavs 1000s better then thee, yea after he had for a season cast thee off, yet his after mercys revisited thee; and he hath not onely pardon'd but cover'd thy sin from the eys of men, though thou be provoking him before many, and giving the Devils caus to blaspheme, that one of his children rebels against him.   And not onely soe but in a word God hath (when thou deserv'st nothing but everlasting confusion) freely given thee Himself, his christ, his grace, yea and all he hath, save onely his glory (which he retains to himself and will not giue to another, yet) that also thou takest from him. ah foolish and wicked wretch! doest thou thus requite the Lord for his bounty. God and all grace might haue gone one way, and thou another taking an Everlasting farewel of one another: but his everlasting loue has made over to thee all that god has, one thing excepted, (which to haue would do thee no good but harme) yet ev'n that, thou art pilfering and stealing from him. should any of those whom thy soul loves, to whom thou hast shew'd kindnes deal thus with thee, would thou take it wel at their hands? yet thou art as vile a clay-heap and a greater sinner then any of them: but god is the King of glory, the fountain of fulness to whom all nations together are less than the drop of a bucket, yea less than nothing. May not heaven and earth stand amazed that thou should deal so with him.

2ly Tis a sin committed with abominable impudency. Amongst men we account him impudent and ridiculous, who having but mean skill, yet hath the face to vaunt of his skill or to bear himself as if he were some body in the presence of an Artist. why this thou doest in gods presence every day; and can god look upon this and not loath the for it? such blind moles as goe up and down the world and see no god in the world, no marvel though they think themselues somebodys, because they see none better than themselues perhaps: But for thee that hast seen the glory off the Lord of hosts, that walkest (or shouldst walk as in his presence continually) for thee to think highly of thy self,! what is this but for the thistle to boast before the Cedar, for a smal taper to glory, before the sun. And can thou see thy self thus doing and not be confounded with thine reproachfull impudency?

Again thou doest hereby what lies in the to frustrate the end of all that god has done for thee: thou endeavourest to make God haue giuen his son out of his bosom, and christ haue giuen himself to the death in vain. For why doth christ saue the by grace, free grace? why least any man should boast therefore 'tis of grace that, so he that glorys might glory in the Lord. And why doth christ redeem thee? why that being redeemed from thy enemys thou might serv him without fear all the days of thy life. wel then, whilest thou servest thy self glory's in thy self what becomes of gods end, which he thought to accomplish with the giving his son to the death? he may lose all that he has bought so dear, for ought that thou regardest it. Nay thou strivest to make him lose it. Gods glory is his last end. now the end is better than the means. god priz'd his glory infinitely more than the world which he made for his glory. Hence, when robbst him of his glory thou doest him a far greater injury than if thou shouldest turn him out of his own world, take it away from him, or utterly spoil and deface it. Nay god prefer'd his glory before the life of his son, it was dearer to him. Hence

(margin: 2ly)

(margin: 3)

(which with astonishment thou might think of, and tears of blood bewayl) so oft as thou derogatest from gods glory, and robs him of that, thou dost more wound him to the heart, then if thou should imbrue thy hands daly in the blood of his son Jesus christ, and wound him with a spear upon the cross.

4ly This is the vilest idolatry that can be imagined   did thou fall down before the sun, moon, or stars, before a dog or cat, why yet this were to adore something.   but adoring some self excellency, this is to worship that which is not, for in me dwells no good thing.   nay 'tis to adore a sinner, an enemy to god, a murderer of my owne soul: One that has bin in some sence far worse than the devil; and therefore better adore him than my self.

5ly This sin makes me likest unto the Devil.   what made the Angels of light become damned spirits, but pride: this sin banish't them out of heaven: am I then an heir of heaven, traveling thitherward, and do I giue it intertainment? It was the ringleader of Sodom's sins, and pull'd down streams of fire and brimstone upon their heads: and do I retain a Sodom within the temple of the holy-ghost.

6ly 'Tis a turning of christ's grace into wantonnes a making of gods gracious gifts to serv my base lust: I fight against the Lord and make him find weapons: the grace he has bestow'd that I fight against him withall.

7ly   Tis also in me a sin against all the dreadful examples of gods judgements for it.   what was sodom's ringleading sin?   they were proud and haughty, and they must fry in flame of fire for it; streames of burning brimstone must wash away the stain of this from off the earth. Proud Pharaoh and his Egyptians must sink in the red sea yea and if Miriam a prophetess will begin a proud contest with Moses she is smitten with leprosie for a warning unto others. Nebuchadnezzar must be driven from among men and eat grass with the ox, till he had learnt this lesson to exalt god and not himself. And Belshazzar his son taken away by a dreadful judgment because he did not learn to humble himself from the example of gods judgement on his father. Herod is smitten of an Angel and consum'd with vermin because he took delight in the peoples over-applauding him.

8ly   It is a sin against the place and persons where I liue. David sins   his heart is lifted up, and 70000 must dy by the destroying angels sword. Hezekiah's heart is lifted up, but wrath comes upon Judah and Jerusalem: all must goe into captivity.   so by my pride I draw downe judgements as with cart-ropes upon the people and place where I liue, and so become an Achan in the camp of Israel.

9ly   This is a grievous sin against myne owne soul. 1 It provokes god to lead me through a howling wilderness of fiery temptations to humble and prove me and shew me what is in my heart. 2ly the pleasing my self with some conceived good in my self keeps me from feeling and mourning under my daly necessity of christ; so that I prize him not cannot long after communion with him, can see no bewty in him why I should desire him. Hence. 3ly. It shuts god and all his grace from my soul. he dwels with the humble and contrite, but he beholds the proud afar off: hence he hides his face from me and I am troubled, filled with disquietment and fears and terrours. hence he is angry with my prayers and graunts not my requests, delivers me not from my sins, but lets them be thornes in the flesh to buffet me, that I might learn to walk humbly with my god. yea he resisteth the proud: hence he crosseth my contrivances, and blasteth my indeavours, and disappointeth my hopes and expectations, and feeds me with the Torment of emptiness, with vexation and rebuke where I hoped to haue met with comfort. so that my soul is overwhelmed with trouble, and I could even roar or make a noise for the disquietment of my heart, but how little kindly melting is there for this my iniquity which causeth it, as 'tis committed against my god?

This is my pride and the fruits of it and if I see so much god sees much more evil in it/

Considerations against sensuality, and delighting more in the creature than in god.

Another principal prevailing evil in my heart is that I cannot prize or see a glory in communion with god, and those solaceings of my self in his love which sometimes god has giv'n me. In the time of my trouble, when creature comfort fail then I fly to god and cry to him arise and save me; but yet again sometimes att the publick ordinances my heart is so leven'd with slouthful sensuality, that it cannot savour or relish the things of god, or the sence of his love let out in a more than ordinary manner. But on the other hand I can lose my heart in letting out mine affections immoderately to creature comforts, and I can find too much sweetness in them. The formidable face of this sin sometimes makes me a terrour to my self   But Lord humble me kindly under it that crying to the for rescue from such a tyrant, it may be possible with god to redeem me from it.

Consid 1.

It argues greatest Atheism. are creature refreshments (which are to day, and gone to morrow, which are daly leaving me desolate and disquieted, as experience tells me, which can comfort no longer than god shines upon them) are those realitys to thee, and the consolations of the holy ghost but a fancy? sure thou deemest them soe. else the loue of a god could not but be more worth, and the sence of it more desireable than all the favour of men, which passeth away like the wind.

2ly   It argues a Carnall, fleshly, sensual, spirit debasing it self below the sphear of a reasonable creature, much more of a son of God. such was the spirit of the ould world that could more savour the sensuall delights, than those spirituall pleasures at gods right hand. and gods spirit was so greeved with them that he would strive with them no longer because they also were flesh: therefore it repented him that he had made man upon the earth: and they were aggravation of his wrath whom he took away with a flood. There is no condemnation to them that be in christ. but who be they? why such as liue not after the flesh, but after the spirit. if ye liue after the flesh ye shall dy saith the Holy ghost. if my soul can live upon sensual contentments, what do I but liue after the flesh?

3ly   'Tis a fayling gods expectation. he might haue Looked that though all my life whilest I knew him not and the good of injoying him why I could liue At eas without desire of him, yet having tasted how gracious and sweet the Lord is, communion with him should haue been more worth than thousands of gould and silver; but I haue both seen and tasted and yet cannot prize it.

4ly   Nay I do dispize it lightly esteem of the rock of my salvation which is foul ingratitude. Among men who can indure to haue their love despiz'd? And shall the God of glory come down from his throne to comfort me when I was almost sinking under the waight of a mountain of lead upon my shoulders? did he put under his everlasting armes and support me, yea did he take off the load of my sins, and take and put me in his bosom to cherish me, giving me to find more sweetness there than ever I found in wayes of sin? and do I thus requite him, to set light by that loue? do I account the consolations of the Lord a small thing? Doe they that dispize common mercys treasure up to themselues wrath against the day of wrath? what treasures of vengeance then, do contemning such speciall grace deserv?

5ly   What greater indignity can be offered to God than to idolize and set up creatures not onely equall with god, but aboue god in my heart which should be his temple. is this to glorify him? Nay 'tis to ungod him to dethrone him. And is not that a traitour indeed, that doth seek to set up a perishing creature in the creatours throne?

6ly   This is spirituall adultery, and it provokes the Lord to Jelousy who hath espoused my soul to himself, that he alone might haue my heart kept chast and my affections intire to himself. But I can intertain dalliance with strange lovers and shut christ my Lord out of dores, and I can let the creature into my affections, but find no room for the god of glory. Not to love christ were an amazing prodigious sin, but to love the creature with that affection which is due onely to christ this were spirituall adultery and falsness in the covenant; but to haue loue to the creature and communion therewith, and not to haue love to christ and fellowship with him: Heaven and earth may be astonished that such a thing should be found in a heart that had ever tasted the sweetness of christ. doth falsness in the Covenant with man deserv both temporall and eternal death? oh then the guilt that this falshood leaves upon me!

7ly This is greatest injury to the creature: to se it self set in gods room   7ly
how would it blush if it were capable of it? how doth the whole creation groan under the burthen of this sin? when thou leanest the weight of thy soul upon it, and would make it a prop to bear the up, it groans under that as too great a burthen fit for the rock of ages onely to sustain.

The relation of Mr Collins[52]

I desire to look at it as a mercy for which I shall ever have cause to bless God that he has pleased to let me live under glorious living gracious dispensers of the Scripture and has out of his grace caused me to be educated under such parents and tutors whose care it was to commend me to be conversant in the holy will and in such duties as they knew God had appointed himself to be set and as continue to be found Hence I had never been suffered to lie at ease in security in my natural estate as those that are out of God's hope and from his ordinances but that from 9 years old and upward the Lord has been working on me sometimes by his word sometimes by his rod to show me what my Christless condition was by nature &c. and that everlasting wrath was my portion as being born an heir of and incapable of avoiding it by anything I was able to do. God's stirrings as had been exceeding frequent though I had been careless as to bring forth fruit answerable thereto so I had not taken such notice thereof &c. which I desire to mourn and be humbled for.

Reading Mister Hooker's book called The Soul's Preparation for Christ[53] it pleased God to let me see I was one needed preparation for him which as it moved me to consider seriously of my condition to resolve to pray and read Scriptures and attend to sermons that I might be able to give account to my parents and to mend my life which was the farthest thing I aimed at So far it wrought with me as sometimes to be asking my parents some questions about my condition and to have some fears and amazement and startling what was to become of me. But after I began to go to school and frequent the company of such as were as careless as myself of any

[52] See note 17.

[53] Thomas Hooker, *The Soules Preparation for Christ* (London, 1632). Thomas Hooker, the founder of Connecticut, was one of the most popular preachers of the time and author of books which were widely read in old England as well as New.

things that considered their everlasting good I began to disrelish what formerly I had savoured and to neglect reading and prayer after that poor sinful fashion which then I used so I had gone and had not the Lord visited me with the small pox which disease was so strong that I thought I should die and I thought I should go to hell remembering how I had backslidden and forgotten God but the Lord was pleased to set me awork to sigh to him and to make me promise another manner of life than hetherto I had done if he pleased to recover me

But after that I soon forgot what I promised and turned aside worse than before   I thought I was going and had now escaped this sickness and need fear no other a great while hence my heart harder than ever hence I began to disrelish God's sabbaths and counted them a burden   All I did endeavour was only to please man I turned aside after other gods and thought repentance would come time enough hereafter   I should but lease these delights which I might have at present and afterward it would be time enough to look after God. My father took notice of it and told me that having had such living affection as I had had certainly the Lord did intend only to harden me against the day of wrath and after I had filled up the measure of my sin God's wrath would seize upon me but this took no effect.

Afterward Mister Hooker preaching out of First Romans 18 here I thought he certainly knew what a sinner I had been what covenants I had broke and seeing I had held the truth in unrighteousness I thought I was as good as in hell already one that had so grievously abused the light there would be no other portion for me

Mister Shepard had a doctrine that here means of grace make not men better there they always make them worse   Here they soften not there they harden   This did exceeding startle me knowing it was my condition but I soon shook that off Ever after on any wooing of God's spirit that truth hath first come to my mind to make me mind my own salvation with fear and trembling   I thought I was one of those whom the means of grace was only for their hardening against the day of wrath.

15 John 22 Mister Shepard he showed that sin against and after clear conviction of sin was a great aggravation of sin and that man had no excuse for it   I thought that my case and therefore there was no cloak for my sin therefore no pardon   God continued this by a word out of 63 Isaiah 20 observed that rebellion against the Lord Jesus is that which grieves the spirit and the grieving of God's spirit is that for which God turns an eye to any man   Some he showed were fugitives that had fled from under God's hand and now like Eve they would not come at him   Notwithstanding that I see my case I had fled away from God and had rather live at peace in my sins than right by God's spirit for my God   Therefore I thought God was become my enemy and nothing to be expected but that he should now come out against me as an enemy and yet this brought me but to a solemn discontented frame of heart I thought I was but travelling to the place of execution

*and therefore I desired to pass away my time with as much comfort and jollity as
I could.*

*My temptation increased so far as to provoke me to murder my self or some of
my friends that so I might be soon brought to an end for this temptation did almost bodily distract me as inwardly distress me   I did not tell the president when
he spoke to me the chief cause.*

*I was resolved to tell nobody but to fill my measure to my self. Afterward that
I might let the president know I intended not to follow his counsel I sent to borrow
an idle book out of the Library &c. I was kept under the lash of Satan's terrors that
he might give me the more easily a false peace*

*And so he did for upon my Admission He soon gave me a false peace those
times that were appointed for God's worship we spent in thinking our own thoughts
speaking our own words doing our own works hardening one another. So I wan-
dered very far after my own devices though he the Lord was not wanting to me by
awakening me in those times when most vile when going farther from him neither
did I or durst I neglect altogether prayer and reading the word yet with so much
formality and hypocrisy as rather increased than otherwise my loathing of them*

*To go read at [undecipherable] 9:ij think not the son of man will come   At
this the Lord was pleased to awaken me yet I thought I had better live securely in
my sins than think of that now   There would come some sickness when I should have
nothing else to do but think of that.*

*Say to the righteous he shall eat the fruit of his doings and so shall the wicked
do too   I found my sins as dear as my life and therefore I had as leave keep the one
as the other. Yet at a private meeting the Lord stirred me again to the repetition of
a sermon out of 6 Genesis 12   At this time the Lord set in with me to show me I
was a son of God by outward covenant yet had corrupted my way   therefore I
thought it just with God to bring distraction on the whole country society congregation that belonged to me and I thought that was the cause of all the crosses they
met with   I thought the Lord might wail over me as a tender father over a
[undecipherable] son &c. This somewhat affected me I thought if the Lord
would send his spirit again I should now change to live inwardly as formerly I
had done outwardly.*

*He hath all power given him that he might give everlasting life to as many as
thou hast given him. I thought I was one that was called for I knew myself to be
a dead sinner but how I could not tell for I argued how formerly I had refused
close walking with God and though all power were given into his hand yet I
thought he had not power enough to pardon my sins so that I not only provoked
God by my sins but sinned against his all-sufficiency in not persuading myself that
he could pardon my sins. When I came home the Lord stirred me up to look over
the sermon again and when I would have prayed I could not I could not look up to*

God   My sins stood all before me   I took up the Bible and God directioned me to the 5 Hosea Oh Ephraim what will I do to thee   Thy goodness is as the morning dew &c. Here the Lord was pleased to show me I had been one whose good melts away like the evening dew that no ingagements or bonds or ties could hold me   Though he had slain me by his prophets &c yet I had dealt treacherous in his covenant therefore I thought if God could not tell what to do with me what should I do with myself   Therefore my condition was exceeding sad.

Mister Sherman out of 13 Luke 7   3 years have I come seeking fruit and found none &c. Such as are to be cut down he showed were impenitent sinners whom God had come seeking fruit but they brought forth none   Such I knew myself and God's former dealings spoke aloud to me   I thought I cumbered to my place God should be exceeding just to cut me down. God also brought to remembrance 6 Hebrews 7 8 9 the ground that drinketh the rain that falls upon it &c. Nigh to cursing whose end is to be burned all my life I knew I had brought forth nothing but thorns and briars   I thought I was under the curse both of the law and covenant and that death spiritual everlasting would soon seize upon me   Satan told me it was too late to pray   My time was past   God had left me a long time and therefore there was little hopes he would return to me again.

Mr shepard sent to speak with me   Hearing how I was he advised me to be constant in private prayer and to be willing to lay down at God's feet that he might do with me as he would. For he hoped that God would have thoughts of mercy toward me though I had carried it still so evil toward me   This somewhat comforted me again   First the Lord forewarned me what should come upon me being at first to a private exposition and God left me to great and gross disobedience to my parents and so to myself he inflicted the greatest affliction that ever I had When I laid so sore wounded it pleased God to show me more of my vileness (when I lay sore wounded) and also to such great pains as God stirred up Mister Shepard to take for me and with me who came and prayed with me and wrestled with God for my life.

He told me of my former carriage and of some sins which I had mentioned to him in private at that time and before yet he wished me still to wait on God and to part with every sin to resolve again constantly to follow God and to seek him The Lord was pleased so far to affect me that I saw something into the nature of sin and what infinite wrong I did to God. When I grew somewhat well and thought how foolish I had been to disobey my parents and put them to so much trouble and grief and myself with so much pain &c. the Lord struck my heart with that sin against thee against thee only have I sinned and done this evil in thy sight   It was to him that I had done that wrong   I had grieved him or else he would have never grieved me thus   I had revolted from him so that I thought that I had infinite cause to bless God and that he had given me time to think of my *sins*   Though I should be lame all my life yet I thought that exceeding easy that I had my life for a prayer. This the Lord continued by a sermon *I pray not for the world*   He showed there were a world of men and women that Christ never prayed for much less died for therefore it stood everyone in hand to consider whether Christ Jesus had prayed for him or no   I knew no provision why Christ should pray for such a poor vile wretch as I yet I thought it were an infinite mercy if he had and I should think my whole life well stood to be given to his glory but I feared he had not

Mister Dunster preached out of ij Matthew 25. 26. *It shall be more tolerable for Sodom and Gomorrah than for these.* He observed where grace abounds in the offer there sin and judgment abounds in the impenitent refuser of it. I thought that for the sins committed in the days of my peace if he should deal with me for those sins it was just with God to let it be a foundation of everlasting wrath to me and if God should let my damnation come on my holding to my sins why I saw it was just with him so to do   The Lord stirred my spirit all the time that that blessed man lived from that least visitation of his and when God took him away he struck me with astonishment as [I] knew my sins had deserved it. I thought if God should now leaved [sic] me to a serious conscience hard heart blind mind it was just with him and indeed so he might do for I desire ever to be sensible of many great out-breakings of my corruptions soon after.

Mr Mitchel mentioned those had especial cause to bewail his death whom God had begun to do some good to by him but the work was left in the midst and I feared God &c. Yet God stirred me up to desire he would not leave his own work in me.

Out [of] ij Matthew 26 the Lord directed me to desire that I might no more turn back and corrupt my doing but might now follow on to know the Lord lest my judgment should be greater than that of Sodom and Gomorrah.

130 Psalms Mister Mitchel preaching out of that   These deeps he showed to be a miserable forlorn estate when those that were in them were too dislocate to get out of them   God showed me I was in such deep such pits as never were in the like   I thought God had laid these as a just plague upon me that he had hardened my heart from his fear and as my soul had loathed him so his soul might loathe me and the rather because I thought God had given me up to his own heart's lust so did I thought I better to be in hell if I could be there without sin than to do God such infinite wrong by my sins   I thought if ever God had thoughts of pardon I should be infinitely engaged to him all my days ij Matthew 27.

He showed all things were committed to Christ that he might show himself

I thought then there was power enough to pardon my sins mercy enough to pity my misery   Therefore if desired he would show forth the glory of his mercy in pardoning such sins as I stood guilty of though it were just with him if he should

not forgive but mark my iniquity yet I thought there was power. When Mister
Mitchel insisted upon that I thought it the best news that ever could be heard that
ever there should be forgiveness for poor sinners   I saw myself so vile that if it
had been better that the whole world should be turned to nothing than God offended
why I thought my sins so great that I dare not think there could be any forgiveness
for them yet I thought if God would forgive me and not only so but change my
vile nature that I might no more sin against him with such reigning power of sin
it would be exceeding great mercy but whether this forgiveness was for me I
durst not apply to myself

    Mister Dunster

    Showed it was the duty of poor heavy laden souls under their sins to come to
Christ for lest [rest?] I thought myself such an one yet the marks he laid down
did not all agree therefore I knew not what measure [word blotted out] of being
laden. Therefore I knew not how to lay hold of Christ. Mister Mitchel laid down
these things that they should live to Christ close with him and to bless him. I suspected my own heart   I thought it would be the greatest happiness to close with
God live to him bless him but I feared my own heart   God let Satan assault me
with great and strong temptations many of which prevailed upon my wretched
heart. I feared all I had done hitherto was nothing but hypocrisy that I was not
elected that I was a dog for whom God had no bread   Many sabbaths past and
came and I got little good but was discontented and sad and was apt to cavil sometimes against the word and against God and thought I was not dealt kindly with
to be kept this long under [one word undecipherable] of spirit and despair but
God gave me then some comfort in telling me that here there was much smoke and
little fire yet God would not quench and that it was my duty to wait patiently on
him and hope in his word and that I might more really and perfectly close with
the Lord Jesus which I did earnestly desire to attend to but so strong were the work-
ings of Satan's cavils and of my own distempers that I think I had sunk away had
not the Lord brought in some relief by that sermon 6 John 35 I am the tree of life
where in the use we were exhorted to come to Christ first from the sense of sin 2ly
from the grace of Christ   I thought if sinners were called to come to Christ and
that should be an argument from sense of their sins then the Lord Jesus would
have me come to him   I thought none labored under so much sin without any relief from myself   I desired though dead in sin to go to Christ to quicken me to
take him as he offered himself to me

    The Lord brought to my mind that place oh wretched man who shall deliver
me from this load of death   If Paul after he came to Christ had a load of sin
and death why then it should not be my great sin that should keep me from Christ

    Remembrance of my sin and the power of it and the breaking it out as Satan was
ready to suggest divers temptation that further distracted me till first John 4

obj.

Mister Mitchel showed we should not be kept from coming to the Lord Jesus by provision of sin for he came for a ransom for sinners He presented me with these 2 things first his own free offers I saw Christ holding out himself freely to me though I had sinned as never any had done Why then should I refuse to come to him and 2ly for Christ's end I thought if I could be willing he should take away my vile heart and change me and help me to live to him I thought then Christ was mine. I heard then we come aright to Christ if we come for life if we desired to be to his honor to live to him I thought I came only to him for life and did desire that I might live to him. I thought I could see myself in some measure weary and heavy laden and therefore I was called to come to him that he might give me rest He told me it was he that took away the iniquity of his people for his name sake I thought it was not the time I had stood out against him that hindered me from coming to him for he set not any time when he said let the wicked forsake his &c. I desired to return to him with weeping and supplication because I had forgot him and I desired to rest upon him for all that grace which he had prophesied for all those that come to him I could not question his willing nor power if I could but get my heart to close with him I desire to be more vile in my own eyes and desired to lay down his hand and desired him to mould me according to his will.

For assurance of faith I can't or dàre not say but I hope I have closed with the Lord Jesus as mine have the condition of the presence wrought in me by himself and further as Christ Jesus is a living Christ and so makes all life to be therefore this life in some poor measure I can see and do truth after that he hath broke the reigning power and dominions of my sins though so many are the outstartings of my heart from him that I have need to go continually to Christ Jesus as the fountain set open to Judah and Jerusalem I desire to keep a continual warfare against all sins I have had hope that I should see the face of a reconciled father in Christ Jesus. I would prize him over everything in this world though I am sensible of my own inability so to do. I do therefore with all all [sic] thanks bless his name that has enwrapt me in any covenant which I do desire to own and to approach to him in society with his people and in his ordinance and there to have communion with him to be as near to him as may be.

Question Do you find it your daily care to walk with God

Answer. I am sensible and desire to be as long as I live as I have many and more perhaps than many others I know there can be no living union without daily command to walking with him living to him I know I can't do so in and of myself but in and by the strength of the Lord Jesus I would endeavour to keep neere to him and if my heart broke away from him why I desire to go to the same blessed [fountain?] for to wash and cleanse and renew me in my spirit I should exceeding question any sincerity if I should find the life of sin and not a bitter loathing thereof.

John Green's Relation./[54]

The Lord began first to awaken me by Mister Shepard's catechize concerning the dread and terror of Christ Jesus coming to judgment   The Lord help me to consider that I was one of those there spoke of   I thought I was one of them and the Lord awakened me to seek him for grace and mercy which I saw I stood need of This consideration much broke my heart   The Lord set me aseeking him in prayer and in reading and I resolved to seek the Lord and follow after him for mercy John French[55] also being in a miserable sickness the Lord was pleased much to awaken me to it and to let me see that I was a miserable creature liable to God's wrath   Considering of all my disobedience to parents my sabbath breakings and my many sins which the Lord help me to mourn for I saw that I was far from God and God far from me.

Mister Shepard spoke in his catechize of man's misery by nature how he was far from God and God far from him   I thought I was one of them   I was an enemy to God and God to me.

Mr Mitchel preaching out of 130 Psalms 2 showing the miserable estate of all unpardoned sinners how God would come to mark their iniquities and set all their sins in order before them I was one of those whose iniquity God would mark if I did not repent   By this God set me aseeking after him in the use off means. God let me see much of the wretchedness of my heart   Sore and sad temptations I had evil thoughts against the Lord. Sometimes I thought none so vile as I none so evil an heart so proud so stubborn so rebellious and I thought God would never show mercy to so vile a miserable wretch as I was. In the consideration of all the mercys that I had despised sabbaths ordinances lectures I thought now that I desired mercy it was just with God never to show mercy to me but forever to loath me and abhor me. Yet seeing myself a Christless undone creature by nature I thought whither ever I went if I did not go to Christ I should perish   Therefore I resolved with myself forever to seek after him and I thought if I did perish I would perish seeking of him. Seeing besides all mine usual sins those heart sins which now I found and felt and those temptations I was under I thought it almost impossible that ever I should find favor with the Lord. Yet the Lord brought that place to me seek and ye shall find knock and it shall be opened ask and it shall be given   I knew not but the Lord might be found of me therefore I resolved to follow him and never to leave him.

But still daily seeing more of the wickedness of my heart how contrary it was to anything that was good seeing I had no power to think one good thought speak one good word that if the Lord out of his free and abundant grace did not come and

---

[54] So numerous were the John Greens of Malden and Cambridge that this one is impossible to identify.

[55] I have been unable to find any record of the John French referred to here.

show mercy to me I was undone forever. Speaking of this to my mother she told me the viler I was the more it was to the honor of God's grace to save me and she did encourage me still to seek him seeing I found nothing in myself I saw my help must be only in going to the Lord Jesus Christ. Know thou the God of thy father serve him with a perfect heart and willing mind &c. Speaking of those poor children that did not now learn to know the God of their father God would come before long in judgment and send them packing to their long home they should see their parents going to heaven but themselves shut out I thought I was one of those finding my heart empty of all good full of all evil. Finding many temptations every day more and more prevailing. Speaking to my father he spoke to me 3 things first if thou canst find really a desire to Christ more than anything tis some sign thou hast some love to Christ but Christ has more to thee

2ly If thou resolve to wait on God as long as thou live

3ly If thou justify God if he should

I thought I desired nothing but Christ to pardon all my sins subdue all my lusts for I had nothing in myself and I thought I had had some resolution to wait on him so long as I lived but yet I found so much evil of my heart that I could hardly believe God could have any thoughts of mercy to one that had despised mercy and abused means of grace as I had done which the Lord was pleased to break my heart in consideration of and let me see an infinite need of Christ to save me out of that estate

I thought of that 130 Psalms. 2. Out of the depth I cried to thee. He showed a soul in the depth of his misery should cry to the Lord I thought I was one myself under the power of Satan an enemy to God and so no way out to perish and had no power in myself to look up to God for help altogether miserable and vile as I was in myself when I went to seek the Lord in secret and to hear God's word and nevermore corruption and temptation prevailing. When I should have got nearest to God then I thought I was farthest from him and thought I grew worse every day than other

Mr. Mitchel preaching out of 130.4. He showed the end of God's forgiving mercy was that he might be feared and those whose desire it was to love and fear him though no power in themselves yet God would have mercy of them I thought it were my happiness that I might fear and love him and sin no more but that I might walk with him in all holy and righteous. I thought I should rather be willing to bear any affliction than such sins to have such thoughts and corruption as then I found and felt The Lord made me mourn under them as the greatest evil and desire Christ as the greatest good all my salvation and hope must be only from the Lord out of his free and abundant grace and mercy to me. Seeing myself thus miserable I had no rest almost night or day no comfort to go about my occasions for I was a miserable Christless undone creature I looked for the fear of God's *wrath to break upon me in this condition that now I was in / yet the Lord brought to mind Christ came not to call righteous but sinners to repentance   I see I was a poor lost undone creature and knew not but Christ might come to call me though nothing in me that should cause the Lord to do anything for me   6 Hosea then shall we know if we follow on to know   I knew not but God might show mercy if I did still wait.*

ij Matthew 29 come to me all ye that are weary and heavy laden   I thought I was in some measure weary and heavy laden that I had no power against the last temptation I thought all the world would not content or give peace to my soul   Only the Lord could pardon my sins subdue my lusts remove my temptations

I thought the Lord was able to subdue my proud heart rebellious will making me lay at his feet able to conquer all my sins and temptations 130 Psalms. I will wait on the Lord and hope in his word   Mister Mitchel showed those poor souls that have these resolutions to wait on the Lord whether he showed mercy to them or no I thought I had had those resolutions seeing all to be vanity in comparison of him

Seeking him daily in use of means in some measure I felt and found power against those temptations whereby I was assaulted which the Lord helped me to loathe myself for and I thought it mercy that I was at all enabled to know any good thoughts for of myself I was not able.

Question was asked while Mister Mitchel preached out of that 130 Psalms when a poor soul might know its sins were pardoned. Answer he that finds power against sin his sins tis a sign they are pardoned   I had found some power I thought which was an encouragement to me yet to seek the Lord and not to leave him.

In the latter end of the Psalm he taught that he that was willing to part with all sin for Christ should have him   I thought I was willing to part with all for Christ to save me from sin and to work all that grace and good I stood in need of.

After this God visited me with the small pox yet I thought it nothing in comparison of the sickness of my soul I had found namely the burthen of my sin I thought I desired no other happiness but to have Christ to walk with him and to him that I might sin no more. But after that I found more violent temptations I thought than ever which made me go mourning up and down the earth and did take my heart off from all other confidence than only the Lord Jesus in whom I see all my hope all my help was. From that the poor and needy seek water I the Lord will hear and help I thought I was one poor needy naked vile stood in infinite need of the Lord Jesus to help and I knew not but the Lord might help me.

5 Matthew blessed are the poor in spirit for theirs are the kingdom of God From thence I thought I was one that was poor in spirit that had no grace or good in me no hope or help nothing in me all my prayers and tears were nothing as they came from me nothing but what might cause God loathe me.

From 65 Isaiah O every one that thirsts come he that hath no manna come I thought I felt that poorness hunger emptiness and therefore knew not but the Lord might call me though not for any desert of mine. // Yet finding much corruption and many temptations yet in my heart and much hypocrisy night evil which I could not believe had it been told me before that I had such a heart as now I see and felt and found that I had to all the Lord was pleased to bring my heart in some measure to subjection to him that I desired to choose him as my chief good to forsake all other things and have no other portion but him alone.

That hath been much comfort to my spirit here we know we are translated from death to life in that we love the brethren I thought those were the men whom I loved above any in the world for what of God I see in them Moreover God let me see more bitterness in sin than ever I saw in any connection and more pleasure in his sabbath and ordinances than ever I found in any sins Those things were once to me most bitter were now made most sweet.

How know you that sin hath been the greatest evil to you.   1 Question

I see sin the greatest for first in that it separated me from all good 2ly in that it offended my God

How can you make it out you love the people of God indeed for there may be love for by ends?   2 Question

I love them for that of God which I see in them and do love their company of all the company I can have in this world

Did you ever see a need of Christ to reconcile you to the father. Answer Yes seeing myself an enemy to God and God to me I see an infinite [need] of the Lord Jesus God man to be a reconciler between God and me   3 Question

Did God ever offer Christ to thee in the ministry of his word and 2ly did thou ever take him. Answer I hope in some measure I have.   4 Question

---

I had thought that if I had such enlargement and such hope then there might be mercy from me. But I heard one speak who made this condition of the covenant if thou hast this much enlargement. Christ requires no portion but mere poverty and emptiness

I thought that there was not such a vile heart in hell as mine and I thought there was no power enough in Christ to subdue such great sins as were in me though there were enough for my justification I was even sinking under the fears of this that there was no hope for me when God brought this to me why art thou cast down oh my soul Jonah's words though I seem to be cast out of thy sight yet I will look toward thine holy temple Why if I perished yet I would desire to perish in God's way.

41 Isaiah when the poor and needy seek water I the God of Jacob will not forsake them 43 Isaiah though thou hast made me to serve with thy sins yet I am he

that blots out thy iniquities for my name sake and will remember thy sins no more. But I thought my heart was not so burdened for sin as it should be. Why said he canst thou have thy heart so burdened for sin as it should be? Now labor to so be odious of thy sin and thy own insufficiency to save thy self and then go to the Lord Jesus Christ to succor thee.

But I have oft called my state in question ij Matthew 28 come to me all that labor and are heavy laden &c. He showed there were burdens of sins and burdens of sorrows and burdens of care and burdens of thy callings   Try thy self saith he which had been thy greatest burden   My heart answered that sin had been my greatest burden. My master told me if I would know whether I loved God or no why there would be fear of him if I loved him I should fear him leave all the world and I should desire him and delight in him more than all the world else which I thought I did.

The consideration of God's great love in sending his son to die for such a vile wretch as I am and considering that in this ordinance we draw nearest to God I thought what shall I render to the Lord   I will take the cup of salvation and pay my vows to the most high and therefore I desire to draw near to Christ in this ordinance but I lie still under a daily burden of sin.

Since I came to New England I heard more of the fullness of Christ than before and this is for empty ones.

At Cambridge

November 18. 1653//

The Lord cast me into a godly family where I was well instructed and called upon to seek the Lord in secret prayer which sometimes I did sometimes I neglected The Lord by Mister Shepard let me see that all I had done could not please God because it was not done in faith I knew not how to help myself   I spoke to my master of that which troubled me   He was glad to see any stirrings in me and bid me labor to feel and to know God if I did seek him in my youth   God took it very well that young ones should give up their first fruits to God. Hereupon I sought the Lord for a time but before long I neglected his counsel and seeking God and attending the good of my soul in the ministry

After this I was to go to sea   I thought that God might reckon with me for all my sins   I was afraid to go   When I was at sea the Lord exercised us with storms and then all my sins came to my mind and I cried to God to hear me though I had thus walked contrary to him to hear me once and if he would this once spare my life I would live near to his praise but when the storm was over and danger past I kept a form of prayer indeed yet I hardened my heart from God's fear like Pharaoh   Mister Shepard showed that the prayer of the wicked was like the howling of dogs and no better they howl upon their beds for myrrh and wine and oil. This much affected me　Hereupon I was assaulted with this temptation why wilt thou pray? But do nothing but sin　I acquainted my master and he bid me of the two evils take the less. After this I heard that Mister Russell's son was propounded　It much sunk my spirit to think I had outsat so many precious opportunities God would leave me to blindness and hardness and take others of my acquaintance.

mr shepard *spoke to this purpose I tell you young persons that have passed your 20 years and slept out your opportunities tis a wonder of wonders if ever God show you mercy　Here I thought God had appended me to be a vessel of his wrath Afterward God refreshed me with the thought of some as Manass that had sold themselves to do wickedness yet God upon their humbling themselves returned them to favor　This gave me hope but I thought that I had lived in place of knowledge and now to be ignorant of God there was no hope for such an one if he went on in sin.*

Mister Shepard showed there were many sons of perdition in godly families and I thought that was spoken to me for aught I knew I was he in that family whom God had appointed to be a son of perdition yet I thought the Lord delighted to show mercy unto poor sinners that had no righteousness in themselves　After this the Lord spoke oft to my heart by that good man but I had caused to be humbled that I had not taken such notice of God's dealings.

After his death I thought God might just speak to me now no more or if he raised up an other why that he should send him to preach blindness and hardness to me yet after this God did speak to me.

130 Psalms　If the Lord take hope to &c. He showed none could stand before the Lord if he married iniquity yet such was the boldness of poor wretches that could stand with all their sins upon them and look God in the face　I thought I was such a bold wretch that was not ashamed before God of all my sins. After God called me to be master of a family and I kept vain company and brought disorder to my family the Lord sent me trouble and vexation and saw it was the Lord's dealing. Another temptation after this presented itself so that I could never forsake my sin and follow the Lord indeed　Sin was not better Christ not precious in thought so that I must now take another course. After this my heart was carried after the world and then God's ordinances were dead things to me and dry　Others could bless God for sermons but to me they were but a mere sound.

Then Mister Dunster out of the 13 Matthew about the stony ground &c. Many poor souls that did for a time grow and live yet had not grace when temptation came they came to nothing these were not fit to come into church fellowship Then I thought that I was such an one that had been called on to come into covenant but I thought I was not fit for such a society so hard hearted a creature I desired that the Lord make me sincere and upright before him to make way for me if he saw good. Afterward I found that my heart was set upon this world and it ate up all that I had heard and I forgot God   After this the Lord showed me what a poor empty creature I was that could not speak one good word or think one good thought   I could not stir up myself to take hold of God in duty yet God had stirred me up to seek him and told me that if I did not seek him his wrath would be on me.

After Mr Norton. We beseech God be reconciled if a man came not to be reconciled to God he did nothing at all   I thought then I had all my work yet to do for I had not been reconciled to God   Hence I prayed daily to God to show me my need   I thought if he would be pleased to save me from wrath and that was not all but to reconcile me to God and that he would make me according to his own heart this has been my prayer and my desire to see my need of him that I had done in some poor measure for my closing with him   I knew not what to say I am in some measure fearful

That gives me encouragement to me [sic] God has bid poor creatures come to him and he would have mercy on them for his own name sake   God helped me to seek him and answered me in some measure

Mr Mitchel on Genesis my spirit shall not always strive with man because he is but flesh. The godly did not allow themselves in their sins as he instanced in some the Lord will help me to see the rich and loath myself for my sin not to allow myself in any sin   I desire he would discover to me more of my wretchedness that at least I might come to take hold of him and make peace with him indeed.

Question.

What experience have you had of the enmity of your heart against God's law? I have found my heart cross to God and his rule because they have crossed some sins of mine that I have been loth to part with   God hath particularly sometimes spoke to me of my own sin and I have been loth to part with it   God help me to see that I [was] under some iniquity which if ever God intended mercy to me he would make me willing to forget and to take him upon his terms which he had offered in his covenant   I shall beset the Lord that no way of wicked might be found in me but that I might put away all the evils of my doings and make him my soul-satisfying portion and that continually. I am a poor ignorant creature that might have known more of him than I have done   I have cause to take shame to myself   I desire the people of God to help me

Question.

Have you ever seen a glory in and had a dear love to God's will. Seeing so much of God in his people at private meetings my heart had dearly loved the people of God. I have found my heart opposed to all that is good and that hath been my burden and a means to make me loathe myself the more.

Question.

Has God never found your heart secretly unwilling to close with Christ on his own terms? Answer. Yes God will not come to me that God might have life I see that the nub of all lay in my will   If I were willing to come to Christ he were willing freely to give himself   I have said to my own heart dost thou desire that the Lord Jesus Christ may indeed be thine for thy self yet I found that I was loth I was loth [sic] to part with some sin that hindered me. But since the Lord hath helped me to part with sin and to desire him to take them away. For of my-self I could not leave them.

This hath been the great stick in my own spirit a great while and I do not so far as I know my heart desire to come in without the people of God see encouragement.

What do you desire Christ for or come to him for? Answer *If my heart de-ceiveth me not I come to him that he would save me from wrath reconcile me to God who by nature am an enemy to him   I know without this I shall never have comfort at the great day   I have thought of this my blood is the chief among* 10000 *I have asked my heart if there were nothing which I have more esteemed than Christ and I have of late found himself hath been most precious to me and therefore have I come to him*   Question.

By coming to him do you mean committing yourself to him resting upon this one thing that prizes a thing another thing to have it Answer. *I think seeking to him is the way to have him.*   Question.

Do you never find a heart that can't prize Christ but had rather walk after the way of your own heart? Answer. *Yes I have seen it many a time but I have considered that was the way to ruin both me and mine after me. I have searched to see whether I loved God's company or no and I have found indeed my opposition against it   Yet I have found in some poor measure that God hath helped me to take delight in his will.*   Question.

When you find your heart dead what course do you take? Why I go to God in *prayer and entreat him to take away that dead heart of mine.* Question. *Do you think it is in your power to obtain it? Answer Yes God* [five words undecipher-able] *and that does much encourage me*   Question.

Joseph champney's relation [56]

Sometimes the Lord has visited me by some illness and then I have resolved to seek and follow the Lord but after recovery I have soon forgot my former pur-poses

After a while the Lord filled me with these words how the Lord would come in flaming fire to render vengeance upon all that know him not that obeyed not his covenant. And that eternity of time should come of misery upon all that know not the Lord Jesus. So that I see it come better to suffer affliction with the people of God than to enjoy the pleasure of sin for a season.

The Lord first discovered my sin in not honoring my father and mother first

---

[56] Joseph Champney, of Cambridge, was made a freeman in 1654, probably shortly after this relation. He died two years later.

Isaiah *The Lord complains of his people that he had brought them up but they rebelled against him* I thought the Lord had done so to me but I had rebelled against him and had not known him *The Lord showed me so much sin in me that I thought myself unworthy to breathe in his air or live upon his earth* I thought it were better for me to die than to live here to dishonor God I thought better for me to make away with myself than to live here to dishonor God and grieve him as I had done but after that Mr Wilson[57] said the Lord took delight in those that sought him early Hence I thought if I sought after the Lord seeing I was but young it may be he would accept of me notwithstanding all. Then I followed after the Lord I thought it were better to forsake all and to seek after a part in God through Christ but when it came to parting with all my lust and ease and pleasure for Christ I thought it hard. But God brought to me this those that forsake father mother house or land for his sake shall have a 1000 fold. Hereby the Lord stirred up my heart to follow him and forsake all I still continued seeking after him and following on to know him I thought to have a part in the Lord Jesus was worth the whole world and more and God helping me to consider of my shortness of time here and of eternity to come. The more I sought the Lord the more he discovered sin Temptations grew stronger but I thought I had more need of Christ Jesus to be my savior. Temptations grew so strong that I was even resolved to give up myself to evil ways and forsake the Lord but then the Lord came and visited me with this that I had heard how that the Lord Jesus offers himself to those that can't save themselves or deliver themselves I thought it was exceeding precious and sweet to me that the Lord should please to come to me at such a time I thought it my blessing to give up my soul and all I had to Christ Jesus and to live here in the land of the living to praise him for his mercy that he had shown me and God encouraged me more by this how that those who follow on to know him shall yet know more of him. Yet I had more discovery of sin and temptations were exceeding strong against me Sometimes I question whether this were the way of the Lord yea or no Once the Lord brought to mind broad is the way that leads [to] destruction and narrow the way &c. And few that find it Now I thought this was a hard and narrow way and further the Lord's way and that which leads to everlasting life yet temptations were exceeding strong and much sin the Lord discovered I thought none so evil as I yet there was forgiveness which the Lord that he might be feared I thought I saw a great deal of God's mercy and goodness I was not able of myself to stand against these temptations that rose up against me Further I saw what need I have of the Lord Christ Jesus every moment I still followed after the Lord. Once the Lord withdrew himself from me and then I thought I was gone but he helped me to seek him that he who

[57] John Wilson, the famous first minister of Boston, was educated at Cambridge and came to Boston in 1630 with the first great wave of settlers.

had been my father's God that he would save me from that wrath due to sin and from sin.

Mr D. preached on those words how when the unclean spirit is gone out of a man he returns again &c. Hereby I was encouraged. But after when he preached on these words again I seeing my woeful state and condition by reason of sin I thought that the unclean spirit were entered into my heart   I thought to go back there was no hope and further after the Lord I must go. My sad condition I yet never made [known] to any   I was ashamed that any should know what a woeful deal of sin was in me at once I told my father of it and he wished me still to seek after the Lord for the Lord would not cast off a soul without he first cast off the Lord

After this I thought that those temptations in a great measure vanished away but when the Lord let me have ease I began to forget the love that he had shown me and the Lord withdrew so that my heart in stead of former softness grew harder and harder   I did not taste such sweetness in God as before. After I heard one show that all pride was abomination to the Lord   Now the Lord helped to see that I had been proud and conceited of what the Lord had done for me and thought that I would not forget the Lord and his mercy to me but after Mr Mitchel upon this return ye backsliding children and I will heal &c. The Lord helped me to consider how I had backslid from the Lord I thought to me the Lord called to return to him yet I thought I saw nothing in me that should move the Lord to turn to me but rather that he should forsake me seeing I had forsaken him yet the Lord helped me to follow after him yet again and I found the Lord returning in his ordinances as before therefore I did desire that I might yet enjoy more of his ordinances if it were his will

---

My wives relation at maldon An. 1657. February 11.

The Lord was pleased to work upon my heart many fears and troubles by the word hearing that preached in the 7 of Matthew 15 every tree that bring not forth good fruit shall be cut down and cast into the fire   It was noted that if the vinedresser prayer and God's patience prevail not with unfruitful trees they must be cut down also that these 3 years I came looking for fruit but found none cut it down &c. The consideration how long I had been under the means of grace God's patience and vinedresser prayer and how many offers of Christ I had rejected not only 3 years but many years the Lord set it sadly upon my heart   I thought I should be cut down for cumbering of the ground so 7 Isaiah beginning it brought forth wild fruit I say cut down the hedge and briars and thorns shall grow there and whereas there is in the same chapter seek and ye shall find that was some encouragement to me to seek though I thought my seeking was as good as nothing yet my desires were that God would show me my sin and show me mercy   Hearing this passage thou hast desired mercy it may be thou art not fit for it I thought it spoke to me I had desired mercy though was not fit for it reading 3 Romans about 19 before there is none that do good they are together become unprofitable I thought myself one unprofitable that could do nothing that was good considering of that Ephraim 2.2. I thought I was a child of wrath by nature even as others   Hearing this from Mister Cotton those that live under the means of grace unconverted are under greater condemnation than are others and that such as are without the favor of god by covenant shall rise up in judgment against them one day I thereupon thought myself under greater condemnation than any others   I had learn in my Catechism how doth Christ enlighten my soul first he convinceth my soul my soul [sic] it is in a wretched sinful miserable estate and that if he continue in that estate he is utterly accursed and notwithstanding he wounds my heart and fills it with terror because he knows not how soon this sentence shall be executed upon him   This was set sadly upon my heart   I thought I was under God's wrath and curse and this filled my heart full of terror because I knew not how to get out   By this and such like things the Lord let me see myself utterly lost and undone without Jesus Christ under the wrath of God   The Lord brought this to mind the Lord commended his love toward us that while we were evil Christ died for us. Also hearing this that this is a fearful saying that Jesus Christ comes into the world to save sinners of whom I am chief. This did much affect my heart to consider God's great love that he should admit of chief sinner's hearing that in public that while God continued the means of grace to me and me to them tis a sign he doth intend to some good   I thought that while God's patience was continued to me [he] did intend me some good yet fearing myself to be still under the wrath of God and being much troubled the Lord pleased to bring to mind that in the first John 1 we have an advocate with the father even Jesus Christ also that in the 13 Zachariah though there is a fountain set open for sin and uncleanness the Lord was pleased much to refresh my heart with that place hoping that he spoke to me and going to a lecture upon the sabbath hearing this same text spoke to if there be any poor sinner sensible of God's wrath and his own misery though thy sins be never so great Christ calls thee to come heart to [three words undecipherable] The Lord was pleased much to refresh my heart so that I took myself spoke to in it. Hearing also this passage if there be any under the wrath of God yet if they can look up to him with an eye of faith he will accept the look of a poor creature toward him. This did much refresh my heart for I thought I found some poor desire toward him. Also hearing that in Joshua ye have backslidden from me yet return and I will have mercy I thought the Lord called me to return to him though I had backslid by my sins also when I considered of God's patience and goodness to me that he continued me yet finding an unbelieving heart much prevailing I heard of that he that believes not is condemned already I went sadly to my heart for *some time yet the Lord was pleased by the word to speak to me by that revelations whosoever will let him come and drink of the waters of life freely hearing this also*

if thou fail but can't come yet come to him that he may draw thee this was encouragement to me in that particular because I found I wanted help to come to him

Where tis said in Genesis I will be a God to Abraham and to his seed this did much encourage me in that he had been the God of my father's and I desired to believe that he would be so to me.

I desire prayer that God would give me more and more rootedness and groundedness in believing.

hARpER ✦ tORChBOOKS

HUMANITIES AND SOCIAL SCIENCES

American Studies: General

American Studies: Colonial

American Studies: From the Revolution to 1860

---

† The New American Nation Series, edited by Henry Steele Commager and Richard B. Morris.

‡ American Perspectives series, edited by Bernard Wishy and William E. Leuchtenburg.

* The Rise of Modern Europe series, edited by William L. Langer.

‖ Researches in the Social, Cultural, and Behavioral Sciences, edited by Benjamin Nelson.

§ The Library of Religion and Culture, edited by Benjamin Nelson.

Σ Harper Modern Science Series, edited by James R. Newman.

° Not for sale in Canada.

American Studies: The Civil War to 1900

American Studies: 1900 to the Present

Anthropology

Art and Art History

History: Modern European

L. B. NAMIER: Vanished Supremacies: *Essays on European History, 1812-1918* ° TB/1088

JOHN U. NEF: Western Civilization Since the Renaissance: *Peace, War, Industry, and the Arts* TB/1113

FREDERICK L. NUSSBAUM: The Triumph of Science and Reason, 1660-1685. * *Illus.* TB/3009

JOHN PLAMENATZ: German Marxism and Russian Communism. ° *New Preface by the Author* TB/1189

RAYMOND W. POSTGATE, Ed.: Revolution from 1789 to 1906: *Selected Documents* TB/1063

PENFIELD ROBERTS: The Quest for Security, 1715-1740. * *Illus.* TB/3016

PRISCILLA ROBERTSON: Revolutions of 1848: *A Social History* TB/1025

ALBERT SOREL: Europe Under the Old Regime. *Translated by Francis H. Herrick* TB/1121

N. N. SUKHANOV: The Russian Revolution, 1917: *Eyewitness Account. Edited by Joel Carmichael* Vol. I TB/1066; Vol. II TB/1067

A. J. P. TAYLOR: The Habsburg Monarch, 1809-1918: *A History of the Austrian Empire and Austria-Hungary* ° TB/1187

JOHN B. WOLF: The Emergence of the Great Powers, 1685-1715. * *Illus.* TB/3010

JOHN B. WOLF: France: 1814-1919: *The Rise of a Liberal-Democratic Society* TB/3019

Intellectual History & History of Ideas

HERSCHEL BAKER: The Image of Man: *A Study of the Idea of Human Dignity in Classical Antiquity, the Middle Ages, and the Renaissance* TB/1047

R. R. BOLGAR: The Classical Heritage and Its Beneficiaries: *From the Carolingian Age to the End of the Renaissance* TB/1125

RANDOLPH S. BOURNE: War and the Intellectuals: *Collected Essays, 1915-1919. ‡ Edited by Carl Resek* TB/3043

J. BRONOWSKI & BRUCE MAZLISH: The Western Intellectual Tradition: *From Leonardo to Hegel* TB/3001

ERNST CASSIRER: The Individual and the Cosmos in Renaissance Philosophy. *Translated with an Introduction by Mario Domandi* TB/1097

NORMAN COHN: The Pursuit of the Millennium: *Revolutionary Messianism in Medieval and Reformation Europe* TB/1037

C. C. GILLISPIE: Genesis and Geology: *The Decades before Darwin* § TB/51

G. RACHEL LEVY: Religious Conceptions of the Stone Age *and Their Influence upon European Thought. Illus. Introduction by Henri Frankfort* TB/106

ARTHUR O. LOVEJOY: The Great Chain of Being: *A Study of the History of an Idea* TB/1009

FRANK E. MANUEL: The Prophets of Paris: *Turgot, Condorcet, Saint-Simon, Fourier, and Comte* TB/1218

PERRY MILLER & T. H. JOHNSON, Editors: The Puritans: *A Sourcebook of Their Writings* Vol. I TB/1093; Vol. II TB/1094

MILTON C. NAHM: Genius and Creativity: *An Essay in the History of Ideas* TB/1196

ROBERT PAYNE: Hubris: *A Study of Pride. Foreword by Sir Herbert Read* TB/1031

RALPH BARTON PERRY: The Thought and Character of William James: *Briefer Version* TB/1156

GEORG SIMMEL et al.: Essays on Sociology, Philosophy, and Aesthetics. ‖ *Edited by Kurt H. Wolff* TB/1234

BRUNO SNELL: The Discovery of the Mind: *The Greek Origins of European Thought* TB/1018

PAGET TOYNBEE: Dante Alighieri: *His Life and Work. Edited with Intro. by Charles S. Singleton* TB/1206

ERNEST LEE TUVESON: Millennium and Utopia: *A Study in the Background of the Idea of Progress. ‖ New Preface by the Author* TB/1134

PAUL VALÉRY: The Outlook for Intelligence TB/2016

PHILIP P. WIENER: Evolution and the Founders of Pragmatism. *Foreword by John Dewey* TB/1212

Literature, Poetry, The Novel & Criticism

JAMES BAIRD: Ishmael: *The Art of Melville in the Contexts of International Primitivism* TB/1023

JACQUES BARZUN: The House of Intellect TB/1051

W. J. BATE: From Classic to Romantic: *Premises of Taste in Eighteenth Century England* TB/1036

RACHEL BESPALOFF: On the Iliad TB/2006

R. P. BLACKMUR et al.: Lectures in Criticism. *Introduction by Huntington Cairns* TB/2003

ABRAHAM CAHAN: The Rise of David Levinsky: *a documentary novel of social mobility in early twentieth century America. Intro. by John Higham* TB/1028

ERNST R. CURTIUS: European Literature and the Latin Middle Ages TB/2015

GEORGE ELIOT: Daniel Deronda: *a novel. Introduction by F. R. Leavis* TB/1039

ADOLF ERMAN, Ed.: The Ancient Egyptians: *A Sourcebook of Their Writings. New Material and Introduction by William Kelly Simpson* TB/1233

ÉTIENNE GILSON: Dante and Philosophy TB/1089

ALFRED HARBAGE: As They Liked It: *A Study of Shakespeare's Moral Artistry* TB/1035

STANLEY R. HOPPER, Ed.: Spiritual Problems in Contemporary Literature § TB/21

A. R. HUMPHREYS: The Augustan World:. *Society, Thought and Letters in 18th Century England* ° TB/1105

ALDOUS HUXLEY: Antic Hay & The Giaconda Smile. ° *Introduction by Martin Green* TB/3503

ALDOUS HUXLEY: Brave New World & Brave New World Revisited. ° *Introduction by Martin Green* TB/3501

HENRY JAMES: Roderick Hudson: *a novel. Introduction by Leon Edel* TB/1016

HENRY JAMES: The Tragic Muse: *a novel. Introduction by Leon Edel* TB/1017

ARNOLD KETTLE: An Introduction to the English Novel. Volume I: *Defoe to George Eliot* TB/1011 Volume II: *Henry James to the Present* TB/1012

ROGER SHERMAN LOOMIS: The Development of Arthurian Romance TB/1167

JOHN STUART MILL: On Bentham and Coleridge. *Introduction by F. R. Leavis* TB/1070

KENNETH B. MURDOCK: Literature and Theology in Colonial New England TB/99

SAMUEL PEPYS: The Diary of Samuel Pepys. ° *Edited by O. F. Morshead. Illus. by Ernest Shepard* TB/1007

ST.-JOHN PERSE: Seamarks TB/2002

GEORGE SANTAYANA: Interpretations of Poetry and Religion § TB/9

HEINRICH STRAUMANN: American Literature in the Twentieth Century. *Third Edition, Revised* TB/1168

PAGET TOYNBEE: Dante Alighieri: *His Life and Works. Edited with Intro. by Charles S. Singleton* TB/1206

DOROTHY VAN GHENT: The English Novel: *Form and Function* TB/1050

E. B. WHITE: One Man's Meat. *Introduction by Walter Blair* TB/3505

MORTON DAUWEN ZABEL, Editor: Literary Opinion in America Vol. I TB/3013; Vol. II TB/3014

Myth, Symbol & Folklore

JOSEPH CAMPBELL, Editor: Pagan and Christian Mysteries. *Illus.* TB/2013

MIRCEA ELIADE: Cosmos and History: *The Myth of the Eternal Return* § TB/2050

MERCEA ELIADE: Rites and Symbols of Initiation: *The Mysteries of Birth and Rebirth* § TB/1236

C. G. JUNG & C. KERÉNYI: Essays on a Science of Mythology: *The Myths of the Divine Child and the Divine Maiden* TB/2014

DORA & ERWIN PANOFSKY: Pandora's Box: *The Changing Aspects of a Mythical Symbol. Revised Edition. Illus.* TB/2021

ERWIN PANOFSKY: Studies in Iconology: *Humanistic Themes in the Art of the Renaissance. 180 illustrations*　TB/1077

JEAN SEZNEC: The Survival of the Pagan Gods: *The Mythological Tradition and its Place in Renaissance Humanism and Art. 108 illustrations*　TB/2004

HELLMUT WILHELM: Change: *Eight Lectures on the I Ching*　TB/2019

HEINRICH ZIMMER: Myths and Symbols in Indian Art and Civilization. *70 illustrations*　TB/2005

Philosophy

G. E. M. ANSCOMBE: An Introduction to Wittgenstein's Tractatus. *Second edition, Revised.* °　TB/1210

HENRI BERGSON: Time and Free Will: *An Essay on the Immediate Data of Consciousness* °　TB/1021

H. J. BLACKHAM: Six Existentialist Thinkers: *Kierkegaard, Nietzsche, Jaspers, Marcel, Heidegger, Sartre* °　TB/1002

CRANE BRINTON: Nietzsche. *New Preface, Bibliography and Epilogue by the Author*　TB/1197

ERNST CASSIRER: The Individual and the Cosmos in Renaissance Philosophy. *Translated with an Introduction by Mario Domandi*　TB/1097

ERNST CASSIRER: Rousseau, Kant and Goethe. *Introduction by Peter Gay*　TB/1092

FREDERICK COPLESTON: Medieval Philosophy °　TB/376

F. M. CORNFORD: Principium Sapientiae: *A Study of the Origins of Greek Philosophical Thought. Edited by W. K. C. Guthrie*　TB/1213

F. M. CORNFORD: From Religion to Philosophy: *A Study in the Origins of Western Speculation* §　TB/20

WILFRID DESAN: The Tragic Finale: *An Essay on the Philosophy of Jean-Paul Sartre*　TB/1030

A. P. D'ENTRÈVES: Natural Law: *An Historical Survey*　TB/1223

HERBERT FINGARETTE: The Self in Transformation: *Psychoanalysis, Philosophy and the Life of the Spirit* ‖　TB/1177

PAUL FRIEDLÄNDER: Plato: *An Introduction*　TB/2017

ÉTIENNE GILSON: Dante and Philosophy　TB/1089

WILLIAM CHASE GREENE: Moira: *Fate, Good, and Evil in Greek Thought*　TB/1104

W. K. C. GUTHRIE: The Greek Philosophers: *From Thales to Aristotle* °　TB/1008

F. H. HEINEMANN: Existentialism and the Modern Predicament　TB/28

ISAAC HUSIK: A History of Medieval Jewish Philosophy　JP/3

EDMUND HUSSERL: Phenomenology and the Crisis of Philosophy. *Translated with an Introduction by Quentin Lauer*　TB/1170

IMMANUEL KANT: The Doctrine of Virtue, *being Part II of The Metaphysic of Morals. Trans. with Notes & Intro. by Mary J. Gregor. Foreword by H. J. Paton*　TB/110

IMMANUEL KANT: Groundwork of the Metaphysic of Morals. *Trans. & analyzed by H. J. Paton*　TB/1159

IMMANUEL KANT: Lectures on Ethics. § *Introduction by Lewis W. Beck*　TB/105

IMMANUEL KANT: Religion Within the Limits of Reason Alone. § *Intro. by T. M. Greene & J. Silber*　TB/67

QUENTIN LAUER: Phenomenology: *Its Genesis and Prospect*　TB/1169

GABRIEL MARCEL: Being and Having: *An Existential Diary. Intro. by James Collins*　TB/310

GEORGE A. MORGAN: What Nietzsche Means　TB/1198

PHILO, SAADYA GAON, & JEHUDA HALEVI: Three Jewish Philosophers. *Ed. by Hans Lewy, Alexander Altmann, & Isaak Heinemann*　TB/813

MICHAEL POLANYI: Personal Knowledge: *Towards a Post-Critical Philosophy*　TB/1158

WILLARD VAN ORMAN QUINE: Elementary Logic: *Revised Edition*　TB/577

WILLARD VAN ORMAN QUINE: From a Logical Point of View: *Logico-Philosophical Essays*　TB/566

BERTRAND RUSSELL et al.: The Philosophy of Bertrand Russell. *Edited by Paul Arthur Schilpp*
　　Vol. I　TB/1095;　Vol. II　TB/1096

L. S. STEBBING: A Modern Introduction to Logic　TB/538

ALFRED NORTH WHITEHEAD: Process and Reality: *An Essay in Cosmology*　TB/1033

PHILIP P. WIENER: Evolution and the Founders of Pragmatism. *Foreword by John Dewey*　TB/1212

WILHELM WINDELBAND: A History of Philosophy
　Vol. I: *Greek, Roman, Medieval*　TB/38
　Vol. II: *Renaissance, Enlightenment, Modern*　TB/39

LUDWIG WITTGENSTEIN: The Blue and Brown Books °　TB/1211

Political Science & Government

JEREMY BENTHAM: The Handbook of Political Fallacies. *Introduction by Crane Brinton*　TB/1069

KENNETH E. BOULDING: Conflict and Defense: *A General Theory*　TB/3024

CRANE BRINTON: English Political Thought in the Nineteenth Century　TB/1071

EDWARD S. CORWIN: American Constitutional History: *Essays edited by Alpheus T. Mason and Gerald Garvey*　TB/1136

ROBERT DAHL & CHARLES E. LINDBLOM: Politics, Economics, and Welfare: *Planning and Politico-Economic Systems Resolved into Basic Social Processes*　TB/3037

JOHN NEVILLE FIGGIS: The Divine Right of Kings. *Introduction by G. R. Elton*　TB/1191

JOHN NEVILLE FIGGIS: Political Thought from Gerson to Grotius: *1414-1625: Seven Studies. Introduction by Garrett Mattingly*　TB/1032

F. L. GANSHOF: Feudalism　TB/1058

G. P. GOOCH: English Democratic Ideas in Seventeenth Century　TB/1006

J. H. HEXTER: More's Utopia: *The Biography of an Idea. New Epilogue by the Author*　TB/1195

SIDNEY HOOK: Reason, Social Myths and Democracy　TB/1237

ROBERT H. JACKSON: The Supreme Court in the American System of Government　TB/1106

DAN N. JACOBS, Ed.: The New Communist Manifesto & *Related Documents. Third edition, Revised*　TB/1078

DAN N. JACOBS & HANS BAERWALD, Eds.: Chinese Communism: *Selected Documents*　TB/3031

ROBERT GREEN MC CLOSKEY: American Conservatism in the Age of Enterprise, 1865-1910　TB/1137

KINGSLEY MARTIN: French Liberal Thought in the Eighteenth Century: *Political Ideas from Bayle to Condorcet*　TB/1114

ROBERTO MICHELS: First Lectures in Political Sociology. *Edited by Alfred De Grazia* ‖ °　TB/1224

JOHN STUART MILL: On Bentham and Coleridge. *Introduction by F. R. Leavis*　TB/1070

BARRINGTON MOORE, JR.: Political Power and Social Theory: *Seven Studies* ‖　TB/1221

BARRINGTON MOORE, JR.: Soviet Politics—The Dilemma of Power: *The Role of Ideas in Social Change* ‖　TB/1222

JOHN B. MORRALL: Political Thought in Medieval Times　TB/1076

JOHN PLAMENATZ: German Marxism and Russian Communism. ° *New Preface by the Author*　TB/1189

KARL R. POPPER: The Open Society and Its Enemies
　Vol. I: *The Spell of Plato*　TB/1101
　Vol. II: *The High Tide of Prophecy: Hegel, Marx, and the Aftermath*　TB/1102

HENRI DE SAINT-SIMON: Social Organization, The Science of Man, and Other Writings. *Edited and Translated by Felix Markham*　TB/1152

JOSEPH A. SCHUMPETER: Capitalism, Socialism and Democracy　TB/3008

CHARLES H. SHINN: Mining Camps: *A Study in American Frontier Government.* ‡ Edited by Rodman W. Paul
TB/3062

Psychology

ALFRED ADLER: The Individual Psychology of Alfred Adler. *Edited by Heinz L. and Rowena R. Ansbacher*
TB/1154

ALFRED ADLER: Problems of Neurosis. *Introduction by Heinz L. Ansbacher* TB/1145

ANTON T. BOISEN: The Exploration of the Inner World: *A Study of Mental Disorder and Religious Experience*
TB/87

HERBERT FINGARETTE: The Self in Transformation: *Psychoanalysis, Philosophy and the Life of the Spirit* ||
TB/1177

SIGMUND FREUD: On Creativity and the Unconscious: *Papers on the Psychology of Art, Literature, Love, Religion.* § *Intro. by Benjamin Nelson* TB/45

C. JUDSON HERRICK: The Evolution of Human Nature
TB/545

WILLIAM JAMES: Psychology: *The Briefer Course.* Edited with an Intro. by Gordon Allport TB/1034

C. G. JUNG: Psychological Reflections TB/2001

C. G. JUNG: Symbols of Transformation: *An Analysis of the Prelude to a Case of Schizophrenia. Illus.*
Vol. I: TB/2009; Vol. II TB/2010

C. G. JUNG & C. KERÉNYI: Essays on a Science of Mythology: *The Myths of the Divine Child and the Divine Maiden* TB/2014

JOHN T. MC NEILL: A History of the Cure of Souls
TB/126

KARL MENNINGER: Theory of Psychoanalytic Technique
TB/1144

ERICH NEUMANN: Amor and Psyche: *The Psychic Development of the Feminine* TB/2012

ERICH NEUMANN: The Archetypal World of Henry Moore. *107 illus.* TB/2020

ERICH NEUMANN: The Origins and History of Consciousness Vol. I *Illus.* TB/2007; Vol. II TB/2008

C. P. OBERNDORF: A History of Psychoanalysis in America
TB/1147

RALPH BARTON PERRY: The Thought and Character of William James: *Briefer Version* TB/1156

JEAN PIAGET, BÄRBEL INHELDER, & ALINA SZEMINSKA: The Child's Conception of Geometry ° TB/1146

JOHN H. SCHAAR: Escape from Authority: *The Perspectives of Erich Fromm* TB/1155

Sociology

JACQUES BARZUN: Race: *A Study in Superstition.* Revised Edition TB/1172

BERNARD BERELSON, Ed.: The Behavioral Sciences Today
TB/1127

ABRAHAM CAHAN: The Rise of David Levinsky: *A documentary novel of social mobility in early twentieth century America. Intro. by John Higham* TB/1028

THOMAS C. COCHRAN: The Inner Revolution: *Essays on the Social Sciences in History* TB/1140

ALLISON DAVIS & JOHN DOLLARD: Children of Bondage: *The Personality Development of Negro Youth in the Urban South* || TB/3049

ST. CLAIR DRAKE & HORACE R. CAYTON: Black Metropolis: *A Study of Negro Life in a Northern City. Revised and Enlarged. Intro. by Everett C. Hughes*
Vol. I TB/1086; Vol. II TB/1087

EMILE DURKHEIM et al.: Essays on Sociology and Philosophy: *With Analyses of Durkheim's Life and Work.* || Edited by Kurt H. Wolff TB/1151

LEON FESTINGER, HENRY W. RIECKEN & STANLEY SCHACHTER: When Prophecy Fails: *A Social and Psychological Account of a Modern Group that Predicted the Destruction of the World* || TB/1132

ALVIN W. GOULDNER: Wildcat Strike: *A Study in Worker-Management Relationships* || TB/1176

FRANCIS J. GRUND: Aristocracy in America: *Social Class in the Formative Years of the New Nation* TB/1001

KURT LEWIN: Field Theory in Social Science: *Selected Theoretical Papers.* || Edited with a Foreword by Dorwin Cartwright TB/1135

R. M. MACIVER: Social Causation TB/1153

ROBERT K. MERTON, LEONARD BROOM, LEONARD S. COTTRELL, JR., Editors: Sociology Today: *Problems and Prospects* || Vol. I TB/1173; Vol. II TB/1174

ROBERTO MICHELS: First Lectures in Political Sociology. *Edited by Alfred De Grazia* || ° TB/1224

BARRINGTON MOORE, JR.: Political Power and Social Theory: *Seven Studies* || TB/1221

BARRINGTON MOORE, JR.: Soviet Politics—The Dilemma of Power: *The Role of Ideas in Social Change* ||
TB/1222

TALCOTT PARSONS & EDWARD A. SHILS, Editors: Toward a General Theory of Action: *Theoretical Foundations for the Social Sciences* TB/1083

JOHN H. ROHRER & MUNRO S. EDMONSON, Eds.: The Eighth Generation Grows Up: *Cultures and Personalities of New Orleans Negroes* || TB/3050

ARNOLD ROSE: The Negro in America: *The Condensed Version of Gunnar Myrdal's An American Dilemma*
TB/3048

KURT SAMUELSSON: Religion and Economic Action: *A Critique of Max Weber's The Protestant Ethic and the Spirit of Capitalism.* || ° *Trans. by E. G. French. Ed. with Intro. by D. C. Coleman* TB/1131

PHILIP SELZNICK: TVA and the Grass Roots: *A Study in the Sociology of Formal Organization* TB/1230

GEORG SIMMEL et al.: Essays on Sociology, Philosophy, and Aesthetics. | *Edited by Kurt H. Wolff* TB/1234

HERBERT SIMON: The Shape of Automation: *For Men and Management* TB/1245

PITIRIM A. SOROKIN: Contemporary Sociological Theories. *Through the First Quarter of the 20th Century* TB/3046

MAURICE R. STEIN: The Eclipse of Community: *An Interpretation of American Studies* TB/1128

FERDINAND TÖNNIES: Community and Society: *Gemeinschaft und Gesellschaft. Translated and edited by Charles P. Loomis* TB/1116

W. LLOYD WARNER & Associates: Democracy in Jonesville: *A Study in Quality and Inequality* || TB/1129

W. LLOYD WARNER: Social Class in America: *The Evaluation of Status* TB/1013

RELIGION

Ancient & Classical

J. H. BREASTED: Development of Religion and Thought in Ancient Egypt. *Introduction by John A. Wilson*
TB/57

HENRI FRANKFORT: Ancient Egyptian Religion: *An Interpretation* TB/77

G. RACHEL LEVY: Religious Conceptions of the Stone Age and their Influence upon European Thought. *Illus. Introduction by Henri Frankfort* TB/106

MARTIN P. NILSSON: Greek Folk Religion. *Foreword by Arthur Darby Nock* TB/78

ALEXANDRE PIANKOFF: The Shrines of Tut-Ankh-Amon. *Edited by N. Rambova. 117 illus.* TB/2011

H. J. ROSE: Religion in Greece and Rome TB/55

Biblical Thought & Literature

W. F. ALBRIGHT: The Biblical Period from Abraham to Ezra TB/102

C. K. BARRETT, Ed.: The New Testament Background: *Selected Documents* TB/86

C. H. DODD: The Authority of the Bible TB/43

M. S. ENSLIN: Christian Beginnings TB/5

M. S. ENSLIN: The Literature of the Christian Movement
TB/6

9